THE

Wildlife

GARDENER'S
ALMANAC

A seasonal guide to increasing
the biodiversity in your garden

JACKIE BENNETT

Illustrated by
Yevheniia Lytvynovych

DAVID & CHARLES

www.davidandcharles.com

CONTENTS

INTRODUCTION

In the context of garden history as a whole, wildlife gardening is a relative newcomer. Like many new ideas, it has taken some time to become accepted by the gardening establishment and for its practitioners not to be considered as dangerous 'alternatives'. My first brush with the idea of inviting wildlife into the garden (rather than trying to keep it out) was in the early 1980s, when I was helping to plan the opening of a new theatre complex in the city of Stoke-on-Trent. The theatre grounds were being converted into an urban nature reserve with ponds, meadows and woodland, providing a much-needed resource for local schoolchildren and theatregoers.

Designed by landscape consultant Chris Baines, it was an incredibly brave and innovative concept at the time – and one which must have risked considerable professional ridicule. The essence of the plan was contained on just four sheets of paper with the headings: Meadow, Woodland Edge, Hedgerow and Water – not the usual terminology of architects. It was nevertheless a very simple but effective way of mentally dividing up a plot of land, be it a domestic garden or a potential building site.

Those four sheets of paper have travelled with me ever since. The basic good sense of the idea of creating landscapes for wildlife, as well as for people, had converted me to wildlife gardening long before I ever had a garden. Nowadays, wildlife gardening is quite a respectable activity and we can all play a part in the revolution that Chris Baines and the conservationists started. But, as with all revolutions, we need a handbook in order to make those ideas work in our own particular situation. This book is therefore first and foremost a practical gardening book – for all those people who are swept away by the spirit of wildlife gardening, but have never quite got round to converting that enthusiasm into reality.

SEASONS AND MONTHS

Under average conditions, the terms 'early', 'mid' and 'late' season as used throughout the book correspond to the following months:

SPRING	SUMMER	AUTUMN	WINTER
Early: March	Early: June	Early: September	Early: December
Mid: April	Mid: July	Mid: October	Mid: January
Late: May	Late: August	Late: November	Late: February

BACK TO BASICS

The secret of making a haven for wildlife, on whatever scale, is to recreate the habitats found in nature. To the four headings already mentioned (water, woodland edge, meadow and hedgerow) I would add wetland, flower borders, compost heap and, most importantly, an untidy patch which is barely 'gardened' at all.

Most gardeners already have some of these habitats although they might not think of them in those terms. Gardening for wildlife does not necessarily mean changing the structure of the garden or throwing out the received wisdom of conventional gardening. There are, however, some key issues to be considered. Chemicals and wildlife, are not, on the whole, complementary. There are some chemical products available which do not leave a residue in the soil and there are those which are designed to be more selective in the pests that they kill. Bear in mind however that every input of chemical, natural-based or artificially manufactured, upsets the balance of pest and pest-eater. Many scientists believe that aphids manage to produce exactly the right number of offspring to support the current population of ladybirds. By wiping out one, we deprive the other of its main means of survival. One of the major arguments for not trying to control pests, is that birds and insects, if left alone, do it so much more effectively.

The most liberating aspect of wildlife gardening is knowing that a little untidiness is a good thing. Suddenly the pressure to keep up appearances is gone and it is socially acceptable to sweep the leaves under the hedge and leave piles of clippings in a corner. Having said that, wildlife gardens do have to be managed.

Native plants are the first choice, not because of some purist philosophy, but because, in general, they support a greater range of species. Nevertheless, birds, insects and mammals are great opportunists and, having established essential ecological relationships with native trees, shrubs and meadow flowers, they will top up their food supplies from any nectar- or berry-bearing plant.

PLANT TYPES

Note that plants are described by their commonly used names (where applicable) as well as by their botanical names. Plants should be considered hardy unless stated otherwise.

ANNUAL: Germinates and flowers the same year, then dies.

BIENNIAL: Germinates one year, flowers the next, then dies.

PERENNIAL: Survives for many years.

BULB: Underground storage organ, developed from bases of the leaves.

CORM: Underground storage organ, developed from the bases of the stems.

RHIZOME: Underground stem.

TUBER: Underground organ, developed from the roots and underground stems.

SHRUB: Woody plant, branching from ground level, usually smaller than a tree.

TREE: Woody plant with a central trunk, usually taller growing than a shrub.

In this book, non-native plants are included if they are particularly useful to wildlife; by the same token native plants, and especially endangered species which gardeners can help to conserve, are included and considered to be 'wildlife'. Strictly speaking, 'native' plants – those which were present in the British Isles before the rise in sea-levels finally separated the islands from the continent of Europe – are a fairly limited group, and since many more species have become 'naturalised' than are truly native, the two are generally grouped together. Naturalised plants may have been imported (accidentally or otherwise) but they behave like natives, thriving in the prevailing climate and soils without human intervention. When we think about creating a wild garden (as opposed to a wildlife garden) we would think only of these native and naturalised plants that take care of themselves. Gardening for wildlife, on the other hand, allows the gardener to draw on a much wider range of plant species, be they native, naturalised or exotic.

One important facet of gardening for wildlife that is sometimes overlooked is the use of colour. Most gardeners employ some element of design in choosing plants in colours that they like or that blend in with an overall colour scheme. For wildlife, and insects in particular, we might make different choices. Flowers may be pollinated by wind and other methods but mainly they rely on insects. The colours and patterns of flowers are not primarily for our benefit, but function as a signalling system to attract these insects: butterflies and flies like yellows and blues, bees prefer blues, reds and purples (which reflect ultraviolet light) and moths go to white. Scent works in co-operation with colour; butterflies seem to gravitate towards heavy scents and bees to lighter, sweeter ones. Moths being night-flying are attracted to those plants which are at their most fragrant in the evening, such as honeysuckle and white campion.

As gardeners, we can be choosy about who (or what) we invite into our gardens. People whose gardens are visited by deer know how quickly a young rose bush can be stripped of its leaves. Others, living in cities, would gladly sacrifice their roses for even the most fleeting glimpse of a mammal of this size. Similar arguments apply to foxes and squirrels. We cannot control nature, but we can to some extent welcome or discourage certain sections of the wildlife population. Conventional gardening books are full of tips to frighten away unwanted wildlife and it is these that the reader must turn to if certain species have become a nuisance. This book starts from the premise that the reader wants to attract a greater range of creatures into the garden.

USING THE BOOK

By dividing the book into months, the aim is to make practical information accessible to the gardener at any time of the year. If, for example, you would like to know which routine jobs should be undertaken in the wildlife garden at a particular time of year, you need simply turn to the 'Tasks for the Month' pages for the relevant month. On the other hand, if you want to locate information on specific plants, habitats, creatures and so on, use the index to direct you to the appropriate pages.

Each chapter is divided into four sections: an introduction to the wildlife and weather to be expected that month, a checklist of the main tasks and instructions on how to carry them out, profiles of plants which are useful to wildlife, and a major practical project for those who want to increase the range of habitats available to wildlife. (For those wanting to find out about different habitats and their value in the garden, the practical project section also provides an overview.) In addition, the Appendices provide information on wildlife gardening with containers, as well as a selection of garden plans, which can be used as a starting point for your own ideas.

In some areas, the seasons may not coincide exactly with those of the book. For this reason, the terms mid-spring and late autumn are used to denote planting and sowing times, for example, rather than specify a month which might be incorrect for particularly cold or mild regions. With experience, gardeners get to know the vagaries of their own climate; but the information in Seasons and Months may be used as a guide for average conditions.

Too many of us worry about the state of our gardens, thinking of them as an extension of the house to be cleaned up and made tidy. I hope this book will help more people actually enjoy their gardens and let the local wildlife judge whether or not they come up to standard.

HARMFUL PLANTS

Some garden and native plants, including their seeds and berries, can be toxic to humans and animals. Check the list of potentially harmful plants on the Royal Horticultural Society website (see Resources) for advice, particularly if you have children or pets.

KEY TO PLANT LISTS

Throughout the book you will find lists of plants for specific uses and these have been coded as follows:

B = Bee plant

C = Caterpillar food plant

N = Butterfly nectar plant

S = Seeds for birds

F = Fruit/berries/nuts for birds/mammals

H = Attractive to hoverflies

I = Large number of associated insects

Nat = Native or naturalised

Po = Poisonous

E = Evergreen

M = Moths

R = Rare in the wild

W = Suitable for wetland garden

JANUARY

One of the best things about a wildlife garden is that winter is a season to be welcomed rather than dreaded. Unlike a conventional garden, where a small selection of carefully chosen shrubs provides artificial 'winter colour', the wildlife garden is rich in its own seasonal plants, birds and animals. Gardeners tend to dislike this time of year, yet this feeling that everything is 'on hold' is part of its charm. If a layer of snow falls, there is little to beat the absolute stillness of a winter's day. Of course, this calm is deceptive and lasts only as long as it takes for the first track marks to appear in the virgin snow. Just beneath the surface, the garden is teeming with life.

Keeping an eye on the bird table from the warmth of the kitchen or living-room is one of the month's chief pleasures. A great cross-section of users should show up, including all the regulars like blackbirds, thrushes, tits and robins. There may also be flocks of migrant fieldfares, redwing or siskins seeking shelter in suburbia from the cutting winds of the open fields.

When the temperature does lift above freezing and the sun emerges temporarily to warm the earth, creatures like hedgehogs, which are normally hibernating, may stir from under a pile of leaves at the bottom of the hedge for a short food foray. Foxes are often seen in gardens during a hard winter, foraging for slugs and beetles. They are not averse to turning over a few rubbish bins either in their search for food.

As for plants, the snowdrop has become something of a cliché for the year. Yet the timing of the flower is perfect; just as we have given up hope of seeing a living plant, it emerges through the melting snow – a constant reminder that this is anything but the dead of winter.

TASKS FOR THE MONTH

- ☐ Start a wildlife notebook
- ☐ Feed birds consistently
- ☐ Keep pond free of ice
- ☐ Draw up plans for a wildlife garden
- ☐ Order wildflower seeds

STARTING A WILDLIFE NOTEBOOK

At the start of the year, make a resolution to record the activity in your garden for one whole twelve-month cycle. Use a hardbacked notebook or desk diary and keep it somewhere near at hand so you can make notes when you come in from the garden. Every event is worth recording, from the appearance of the first snowdrop to the last holly berry disappearing in the beak of a visiting fieldfare.

Keeping a notebook is not just a pleasant exercise, it will also help you to plan next year's garden and monitor changes in the frequency and behaviour of local wildlife. It doesn't need to be elaborate or a literary masterpiece, just the date and a few notes will do. As the garden develops and the range of species increases, it will provide a lasting record not only for your own use, but perhaps for future owners of your house and garden.

LOOKING AFTER THE BIRDS

This is probably the month during which garden birds benefit most from a little human intervention. Natural food sources like windfallen apples and hawthorn berries have been used up by the population of local birds, in competition with visitors from the Arctic north who take refuge in gardens at this time of year. Insects are in hibernation, the ground is frozen solid and water sources are iced over. It is therefore vital to feed birds regularly, putting out food every day. Early morning is the best time, although you can put out a second 'feed' in the early afternoon. Fresh water is important too, even if you have a pond – many birds will drink from the bird table and wash their feathers in the pond.

Put out a range of food, on the ground and on the table (see the practical project for December for advice on choosing a bird table). Include hanging feeders with nuts for tits, sparrows and rarer visitors like siskins; apples on the ground for blackbirds and thrushes; and seeds, nuts and fat on the table for robins, starlings and other species. They will come to rely on this food supply, so once you've begun to feed keep it up until the worst of the winter is over.

RECOMMENDED BIRD FOOD

Peanuts These should be good quality, dry, unsalted nuts designed for bird feeding. Use a mesh hanging bird feeder so that whole nuts cannot be fed to baby birds. A sturdy squirrel proof feeder is also a good idea. Avoid nuts that show signs of mould – peanuts can contain aflatoxin which can be fatal to birds.

Seed mixes Wild bird food mixtures containing sunflower and other seeds are available from suppliers advertising in bird magazines and, increasingly, from hardware and pet shops. Black sunflower seeds are particularly high energy.

Kitchen scraps Not all food scraps are suitable. Try suet, dry porridge oats, cheese, apples and sultanas or raisins – soaked in water to make them soft. Stale bread or cake is acceptable but it should be soaked in water to make it easier to swallow.

Bird Cake Recipe

- Suet or lard, softened

- Dry mixture: bird seeds, nuts, oats and dried fruit. Use approximately 1 part fat to 2 parts dried mixture

- A mould: a small bowl or empty plastic cartons

In a bowl, mix the dry ingredients with the fat until it all sticks together. Spoon the mixture into the mould(s). Leave to set in a cool place (or fridge) and then tip out onto the bird table. Keep away from dogs and other pets.

DISCOURAGE SCAVENGERS
Do not leave uneaten bird food out overnight as it can attract rats and mice.

KEEPING THE POND ICE FREE

It is important to keep at least some part of the pond free of ice throughout any cold spells. This not only allows birds and other visitors like foxes to drink but also stops a build-up of gases under the ice. As organic matter decomposes gases are released which, if trapped by a layer of ice, will build up and poison existing pond life. A simple and cheap method of allowing the pond to 'breathe' is to float a block of wood on the surface of the water. Then, when the pond freezes remove the wood, leaving a gap. A child's plastic or foam ball will also prevent ice forming over all the surface, but avoid lurid colours which can scare away potential users.

MAKING PLANS

This is the best month for planning out a new garden layout (see Appendix 2 for suggested plans). Even if you only envisage a few minor changes, it is a good idea to try them out on paper beforehand. If you are starting with a bare plot or considering a fairly major project like digging a pond or planting a mini-woodland, it is essential to think it through in some detail before you ever put spade to earth.

Consider first of all which features already in the garden are useful to wildlife – mature trees, for instance, a compost heap or a pond of some kind. Use the Essential Features list to identify elements you want to keep. Draw a rough plan of the garden and mark in these features. Next, decide which features could be improved to make them more wildlife friendly, such as adding stepping stones to a steep-sided pond or replanting an existing border with nectar-rich flowers. You might wish to turn part of the lawn over to a wildflower meadow but, before you do, consider which areas it would be practical to grow long and which parts you really need to keep as a conventional lawn. Be prepared to play around with this plan – all winter if you have to. Try all sorts of combinations, bearing in mind how much work they will involve, until you are happy that the layout is one that will suit you and your lifestyle, as well as the needs of the wildlife you want to attract.

Essential Features

☐ Pond

☐ Marsh/bog area

☐ Mature living trees

☐ Old hollow/fallen trees

☐ Young trees

☐ Climbing plants

☐ Native mixed hedge

☐ Compost heap/bin

☐ Bird table

☐ Bird/bat boxes

☐ Berry-bearing shrubs

☐ Nectar-rich flowers

☐ Untidy corner

☐ Long grass/meadow area

ORDERING WILDFLOWER SEEDS

Many native species are not yet available as pot-grown plants in garden centres. This means that there is no option but to grow some varieties from seed, which is more readily available. Check out the seed packet displays in supermarkets and garden centres and online seed suppliers.

Annual flowers are particularly easy to grow and they don't necessarily have to be native as long as they are colourful and nectar-rich. Night-scented stocks, cornflowers, candytuft, snapdragons and sunflowers will attract insects and therefore increase the range of birds that visit the garden. Half-hardy annuals and biennial plants can also be raised from seed and incorporated in borders, where they will act as a magnet in the summer months to bees and butterflies.

If space is a problem, hardy and half-hardy annual seeds can be sown directly into large pots, where they can be left to grow on to full size. The pots can then be moved around the patio to create instant colour.

RECOMMENDED FLOWER SEEDS

HALF-HARDY ANNUALS

African marigold (*Tagetes erecta*) N, B
French marigold (*Tagetes patula*) N, B
Heliotrope (*Heliotropium*) N
Petunia N
Tobacco plant (*Nicotiana*) N

HARDY ANNUALS

Candytuft (*Iberis umbellata*) N
Common poppy (*Papaver rhoeas*)B, H, Nat
Corncockle (*Agrostemma githago*) N, Po, Nat
Corn chamomile (*Anthemis arvensis*) N, Nat
Cornflower (*Centaurea cyanus*) N, B, Nat
Larkspur (*Delphinium consolida*) B, Po, Nat
Love-in-a-mist (*Nigella damascena*) N
Mignonette (*Reseda odorata*) N, C
Nasturtium (*Tropaeolum majus*) H, C
Night-scented stock (*Matthiola bicornis*) N, M
Poached egg flower
(*Limnanthes douglasii*) B, H
Pot marigold (*Calendula officinalis*) B, H
Sunflower (*Helianthus annuus*) N, B, S
Virginia stock (*Malcolmia maritima*) N, B

BIENNIALS

Evening primrose (*Oenothera biennis*) B, H, M
Forget-me-not (*Myosotis sylvatica*) N, B, Nat
Foxglove (*Digitalis purpurea*) B, Po, Nat
Great mullein (*Verbascum thapsus*) B, Nat
Sweet rocket (*Hesperis matronalis*) N, Nat
Sweet william (*Dianthus barbatus*) N
Teasel (*Dipsacus fullonum*) N, B, S, Nat
Wallflower (*Cheiranthus cheiri*) N, Nat

Plants of the Month

COMMON SNOWDROP
(Galanthus nivalis)

The common snowdrop, found widely in damp woodlands, on banks and in hedgerows, provides the first flowers of the year. A pretty plant which looks best planted in natural 'drifts'.

TYPE Bulb

FLOWERS White, inner petals tipped with green, mid-winter to early spring

HEIGHT 13–20cm (5–8in)

PLANTING Snowdrops establish best when planted 'in the green' in early spring – when they still have leaves

SITE Partly shaded. In grass, under trees, shrubs or hedges

SOIL Any, but grows best of all in rich, moist soils

CARE May take two to three years to get established but needs no attention

PROPAGATION When the clumps outgrow their space, lift and divide the bulbs immediately after flowering

VARIETIES 'S. Arnott' is a larger, sweetly scented hybrid; 'Viradpice' has green markings on the outer petals too

WILDLIFE The scent acts as a signal to insects waking up prematurely from hibernation. On warm days, when there are more likely to be insects about, the petals open to their fullest

WINTER-FLOWERING HONEYSUCKLE
(Lonicera fragrantissima)

The winter-flowering honeysuckle is not native to Britain (unlike the wild honeysuckle or woodbine, *L. periclymenum*) but it is well worth growing for its fragrant flowers and foliage cover.

TYPE Partly evergreen climbing shrub

FLOWERS Creamy white, early winter to early spring

HEIGHT 1.8m (6ft)

PLANTING Plant in mid- to late spring, against walls, fences or trellis, or in containers

SITE Sun or light shade – ideally the roots should be in shade and the top in sun

SOIL Any well-drained soil

CARE Mulch around the plant with leaf mould or compost in spring. Regular pruning is not necessary, but straggly or overgrown plants should have old wood removed after flowering

PROPAGATION Stem cuttings in mid- to late summer

RELATED *L. standishii* is similar but grows to a more compact 1.2m (4ft)

WILDLIFE The foliage may provide cover for birds and the flowers are welcoming to insects when the rest of the garden is bare

VIBURNUM
(Viburnum x bodnantense)

This early flowering member of the viburnum family is a hardy species bearing clusters of flowers on bare wood even in the hardest winter.

TYPE Deciduous shrub

FLOWERS White flushed with pink, throughout winter

HEIGHT 3m (10ft)

SPREAD 2.75m (9ft)

PLANTING Plant from mid-autumn to early spring, adding some garden compost or well-rotted manure to the planting hole

SITE Full sun or light shade

SOIL Moist, fertile

CARE No regular pruning needed, but if the shrub becomes overgrown, thin out in mid-spring

PROPAGATION From cuttings in late summer to early autumn

WILDLIFE Flowering shrubs are few and far between this month and the blooms of Viburnum x bodnantense have a particularly good perfume to attract insects

WINTER ACONITE
(Eranthis hyemalis)

Originally an introduction from Europe and Asia, this member of the buttercup family is naturalised in many parts of Britain and widely grown in gardens. The dazzling yellow flowers appear before or at the same time as snowdrops.

TYPE Tuber

FLOWERS Bright yellow, mid-winter to early spring

HEIGHT 10cm (4in)

PLANTING Plant tubers in late summer, 3–5cm (1–2in) deep and 8cm (3in) apart in groups of six or more

SITE Sun whilst flowering, partial shade for the rest of the year. Under deciduous trees or between shrubs

SOIL Moist, humus-rich, leaf mould

CARE No special care needed

PROPAGATION Plants will naturally set seed and spread. Alternatively, lift and divide tubers immediately after flowering

WILDLIFE Provides early pollen for waking insects. The winter aconite relies on flies and bees for pollination

PRACTICAL PROJECT

PUTTING UP BAT BOXES

WHY ENCOURAGE BATS?

Many species of bats are becoming rare and in some cases nearing extinction because of disturbance and loss of natural roost sites. In cities and intensively farmed areas, their food supply of insects is also becoming depleted. A healthy garden with a wide range of insects will provide a rich night-time hunting ground. By eating a large proportion of pests like midges, the bats will help to maintain the garden's natural balance.

By understanding bats' natural cycle we can choose the best ways to encourage them to use our gardens and houses. Bats traditionally roost in hollow trees or in caves, but have increasingly become adapted to buildings. For winter hibernation they will seek out a well-insulated spot with a constant temperature but it is quite difficult to provide these conditions artificially. During the rest of the year, bats are less particular and will use a number of different sites. In spring they will seek out a safe place to give birth and rear their young. In summer they may choose a cooler spot to roost and in autumn a slightly warmer one. If your garden has any old trees they may well be inhabited by bats. If not, it is even more important to put up bat boxes.

WHAT TO CONSIDER

A bat box works on the same principle as a bird box except that instead of a hole at the front for access, there is a small gap underneath which needs to be wide enough for the bats to enter, but small enough to keep out predators such as cats.

Buy a proprietary bat box from one of the wildlife organisations (see Resources). These are constructed of untreated timber or other safe materials and have a rough surface that allows the bat to cling to the interior. A large 'landing' plate is useful to guide the bat into the box.

SITING THE BOX

Position bat boxes at 3–5m (10–15ft) above ground (or higher), on a tree, post or on the house wall. Make sure the bats have a clear flight path by removing overhanging branches or other obstructions. If possible site three boxes facing south, south-west and south-east. This will enable bats to select the most suitable roost for the time of year. Avoid siting boxes near lights that come on after dark, as bats find artificial light disturbing.

FIXING THE BOX

The box can be nailed onto a wooden post or tree. If attaching to brickwork, use rawlplugs and screws.

AFTERCARE

Once in situ, leave the box undisturbed. A special licence is required to disturb or handle bats. If you need advice on any aspect of bat behaviour contact the Bat Conservation Trust (see Resources).

BAT ROOSTS

Bats use a range of natural and manmade places as roosts and some species such as the Greater and Lesser Horseshoes will not use bat boxes at all. A healthy garden with plenty of insects and night scented plants will attract bats if they are in the vicinity. A pond is another major attraction that will help to encourage bats.

BAT FACTS

THE LAW AND BATS

Bats and their roosts are protected by law and it is an offence to disturb roosting bats. If you have bats in your roof space, cellar or any part of your property, you should contact the Bat Conservation Trust (see Resources) for advice.

EXTINCTION

In 1990 the greater mouse-eared bat was officially declared extinct – the first mammal to become extinct in the British Isles for 250 years. There have been reports of this bat making a return to the south of England, although the plight of many bats continues to be precarious.

BAT SPECIES

COMMONLY SEEN IN GARDENS AND AROUND HOUSES

Brown long-eared

Daubenton's (especially near ponds and canals)

Natterer's

Noctule

Pipistrelle

Serotine (common in the south of England)

RARELY SEEN

Barbastelle

Bechstein's

Brandt's

Greater and lesser horseshoe

Grey long-eared

Leisler's

Whiskered

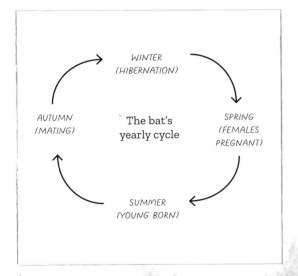

The bat's yearly cycle

WINTER (HIBERNATION)

SPRING (FEMALES PREGNANT)

SUMMER (YOUNG BORN)

AUTUMN (MATING)

FEBRUARY

Typically, this is a wet and bitterly cold month with more than its fair share of snow and ice. Fortunately, the weather does not make all wildlife inactive and in the early morning it is quite possible to see fox and badger tracks, made during the previous night, as they find mates and make preparations for the birth of their cubs.

Resident birds will also be gearing up for the breeding season. An early morning chorus of robins, blackbirds and thrushes signals the increasing interest males and females are taking in one another as they noisily advertise for mates. In a small garden it is unusual to have more than one pair of any particular species nesting, simply because the males will defend their territory against incomers of the same species. Even in mild weather birds are still reliant on supplementary food from the bird table, particularly the females who are building up their strength for breeding. Frogs and toads are beginning to emerge from hibernation, although if the weather is extremely cold they will stay out of sight for another month. Butterflies, particularly brimstones and commas, may be stirred into life by a spell of weak sunshine.

This is the month that catkins begin to appear on the branches of hazel and alder trees. Hazel catkins are known colloquially as 'lambs' tails', making a connection in our minds between the first sight of these flowers and the beginning of a new seasonal cycle. Beneath the trees, celandines, sweet violets, spring crocus and snowdrops are making a carpet of scent and colour, offering sustenance to waking insects and setting the scene for spring.

TASKS FOR THE MONTH

- [ ] Continue feeding birds
- [ ] Prune Buddleia davidii
- [ ] Cut back overgrown berberis and cotoneaster
- [ ] Lift and divide perennial border plants
- [ ] Prune shrub roses
- [ ] Plant lily of the valley
- [ ] Trim back perennials

FEEDING BIRDS

Continue putting out food and water on the bird table, particularly during cold spells (see January for tips on feeding). This is also a good month to put up nesting boxes that garden birds will use during the spring.

PRUNING BUDDLEIA

Buddleia davidii bushes may be pruned this month. Strictly speaking, buddleia does not need to be pruned – witness the hundreds of thousands of garden escapees growing untended on urban wasteland. However, bushes which have outgrown their space or produced a poor show of flowers will benefit, producing strong new stems and, more importantly, large clusters of flowers for the butterflies.

Cut back all last year's shoots to within 5 or 8cm (2 or 3in) of the old wood. In mild winters, new rosettes of leaves may already have started to form at the junction of the old and new wood and these should be left undamaged.

PRUNING BERBERIS AND COTONEASTER

Barberry (Berberis) and cotoneaster shrubs, both of value for their berries, can be cut back to prevent them becoming too overgrown and woody. The thicker, tougher three-year-old stems (or older) are cut out at ground level, opening up the plant to allow more light and air to the centre.

Using sharp secateurs, prune the old wood back to within about 10cm (4in) of the ground.

MOVING TREES AND SHRUBS

This is the last month for lifting and replanting shrubs or trees which may be in the wrong position. By spring, nest building will be underway, and moving established plants can be very disruptive. If the ground is too hard or the weather bad, leave until autumn.

LIFTING AND DIVIDING BORDER PERENNIALS

Hardy perennial plants which have been in place for three years or more can be lifted and divided now to make new plants. All the species listed in Perennials to Divide are good for wildlife, and this is the simplest method of propagation. (Division can also be done in autumn.)

• Prepare the ground where the new plants are going to be put, by digging over and adding some garden compost.

• Using a fork, gently work the clump out of the ground, taking care not to break the roots.

• For large clumps, insert two forks, back to back, into the centre of the clump and prise the roots apart. Small clumps can be pulled apart by hand.

• Select small, healthy pieces from the outside of the plant with at least three or four young shoots, for replanting. The central woody portion can be discarded. The new sections can be planted immediately, allowing enough room between plants for development to their full size.

PRUNE SHRUB ROSES

The species shrub roses can be pruned now that the hips have been safely eaten during the winter months and while the plant is still dormant. Wild and species roses, whether grown as hedging or as shrubs, do not need annual hard pruning like the hybrid bush roses, but from time to time they will benefit from a light 'tidying up' – perhaps every three or four years. Dog rose (*Rosa canina*), sweet briar (*Rosa rubiginosa*), *Rosa rugosa*, *Rosa x alba*, and *Rosa glauca* can all be treated in the same way.

• Using sharp secateurs, first cut out any old, dead or diseased stems at ground level.

• Cut back any long straggly stems to one third of their length to keep the plant tidy.

• Finally, snip off several centimetres (a few inches) from the tips of all the stems to encourage side shoots, which will bear flowers in later years.

SHRINKING VIOLETS

One of our plants of this month is the sweet violet, but the population of some violet species is dwindling. Always buy seeds and young plants from nurseries, never collect from the wild. The Teesdale violet (V. nepestris) is found only in Upper Teesdale and at a single site in Cumbria. Likewise, the fen violet (V. persicifolia) is confined to a few scattered locations in East Anglia.

PLANTING LILY OF THE VALLEY

Lily of the valley (*Convallaria majalis*), best known for the delicious fragrance of its white, bell-shaped flowers, is so widely planted in gardens that it is sometimes forgotten that it is a native of our woodlands, although not so widespread in the wild as it used to be. It spreads rapidly if given the right conditions and makes an excellent woodland floor plant for a wild part of the garden. Existing clumps can be divided now or individual crowns can be bought from nurseries.

• Choose a shady spot with moist soil into which some leaf mould has been added.

• Plant the crowns point upwards, 8–10cm (3–4in) apart. They should lie just beneath the surface of the soil. Clumps of crowns can be placed 15cm (6in) apart.

• Water in well.

TRIMMING BACK PERENNIALS

Border perennial plants which were not cut back in autumn (leaving the stems for over-wintering insects) should be trimmed now to make room for new growth. Cut off any dead or straggly stems to just above ground level with secateurs. In mild winters, young leaves and stems will already be appearing. Removing the old growth rejuvenates the plants and allows these new leaves and stems plenty of room to grow. Add the cuttings to the compost heap.

SHY-FLOWERING LILIES

One of the reasons lily of the valley often fails in gardens is that it is planted in dry, open, sunny beds, when it really needs a moist soil and the cover of deciduous trees.

PERENNIALS TO DIVIDE

Globe thistle (*Echinops ritro*) B, N

Golden rod (*Solidago canadensis*) B, N

Greater knapweed (*Centaurea scabiosa*) B, N, Nat

Michaelmas daisy (*Aster nova-belgii*) N

Sedum (*S. spectabile* and 'Autumn Joy') N

Yarrow (*Achillea millefolium* and *A. filipendulina*) B, N, Nat

Plants of the Month

ALDER (*Alnus glutinosa*)

The tall-growing native alder is happiest beside a freshwater river or stream, but it is also very adaptable to garden sites. It is very useful in cities and towns because of its resistance to air pollution but is only suitable for very large gardens.

TYPE Deciduous tree

FLOWERS Catkins appear in late winter/ early spring. Male catkins are long and yellow; females are round and purplish

HEIGHT 10–15m (30–50ft)

SPREAD 3m (10ft)

PLANTING Plant young trees from mid-autumn to early spring

SITE In a marshy area or at the back of a woodland belt

SOIL Prefers damp, waterlogged soil

CARE No special care needed

PROPAGATION From seed collected in autumn

VARIETIES *A. glutinosa* 'Imperialis' is smaller and slower growing – more suitable for average-sized gardens

WILDLIFE There are around ninety insect species associated with alder, including the alder fly and alder moth. As the weather warms up the male catkins open and disperse a cloud of pollen to fertilise the female catkins. In autumn and winter the tree is a good source of seed for siskins, redpolls and other small birds

HAZEL (*Corylus avellana*)

An ancient native shrub that forms thickets in the wild and bears the distinctive 'lambs'-tails' catkins and edible hazelnuts or cobnuts. Traditionally coppiced to produce flexible lengths suitable for woven fencing and basket making.

TYPE Deciduous shrub

FLOWERS Catkins in late winter. Male catkins are yellow; female are tiny red tassels

HEIGHT 4–6m (12–20ft)

SPREAD 5m (15ft)

PLANTING Plant young trees between mid-autumn and early spring

SITE Sunny or partly shaded. In a shrub border or amongst larger trees

SOIL Any well-drained soil

CARE No pruning required. If planted as part of a mini woodland, hazel can be coppiced (regularly cut back to ground level so that new straight shoots are sent out from the base), allowing more light to the woodland floor. In the autumn, collect nuts when the husks have turned brown and store in a dry, airy place

PROPAGATION By seed collected in the autumn

VARIETIES Corkscrew hazel (*C. avellana* 'Contorta') is a good alternative for a small garden. It has the same yellow catkins, but it is slow-growing and will only reach 2.5m (8ft) in height. The stems are twisted, hence the name

WILDLIFE At this time of year, wind causes the catkins to release pollen, for the benefit of early foraging bees and insects. In autumn, squirrels and field mice add the nuts to their winter store

STINKING HELLEBORE
(Helleborus foetidus)

The stinking hellebore
earned its name from
the seed pods which
produce an acrid smell
when crushed, although
certainly not as
unpleasant as the name
suggests. Although
quite rare in the wild, it can be found in
old woodlands on chalky soils. The unusual
pallid flowers and dramatic leaves make
it an interesting garden plant and a useful
supply of early nectar.

TYPE Perennial, evergreen

FLOWERS Yellow-green with purple rim,
late winter to mid-spring

HEIGHT 60cm (24in)

PLANTING Plant pot-grown plants
in autumn

SITE Shade

SOIL Dry, chalky

CARE Leave undisturbed

PROPAGATION From seed in summer

RELATED The green hellebore
(Helleborus viridis) also flowers this
month and can be distinguished by the
wholly green flowers, without the purple
edging. It is smaller, only 45cm (18in) high,
and it prefers a moist soil. The leaves are
deciduous, dying back in summer

WILDLIFE A ready source of nectar for
early honey and bumble bees. H. viridis
flowers a couple of weeks later than H.
foetidus, so by planting both, a continuous
supply of nectar is assured

SWEET VIOLET (Viola odorata)

A widespread native
flower, the sweet-smelling
violet grows naturally on
banks, in copses and in
hedgerows. In the garden
it will adapt to any shady
location, in grass under
trees, under hedges or
in the border. Its relative,
the common dog violet
(Viola riviniana) is unscented and flowers later,
but is also a useful wildlife plant, supplying
nectar for spring broods of butterfly.

TYPE Perennial

FLOWERS Dark violet, sometimes white, late
winter to mid-spring; occasionally in autumn

HEIGHT 10–15cm (4–6in)

SPREAD 30cm (12in)

PLANTING Plant out in early autumn or late
spring, 30cm (12in) apart

SITE Partial shade

SOIL Any

CARE No special care needed

PROPAGATION Plants spread naturally by
runners. These can be rooted in summer or the
whole plant can be divided in autumn

VARIETIES A range of colours are available in
the garden varieties; 'Coeur d'Alsace' is a rich
pink and 'Sulphurea' is a yellow form

WILDLIFE This is the earliest flowering of the
native violets and provides nectar for flying
insects and food for butterfly caterpillars,
particularly the fritillary family

MAKING AND SITING NEST BOXES

Birds need safe places to raise their young in the spring and summer, and gardens provide some of the best habitats. If possible there should be a choice of potential sites that different species can use – thick hedgerows for sparrows, walls covered by climbers for blackbirds and thrushes, hollow tree trunks for blue tits, and sheds and outbuildings for robins and swallows. Nest boxes should be thought of as an adjunct to these natural sites, not a replacement for them. In towns, where trees are scarce, or in brand new gardens, nest boxes are vital and it is worth trying to include several different types in various positions.

CHOOSING A BOX

The type of bird you want to attract will determine the type of nesting box – anything from a simple wooden ledge to a large owl box. The ones made from wood, in natural colours, are preferable as they will not advertise the birds' location to potential predators. Don't site the box near feeding tables as it is very unlikely that a bird would nest in such a prominent position.

SITING THE BOX

Try to put the box in view of a window, so you can watch the occupants without disturbing them. It should be put at least 3m (10ft) from the ground, out of reach of cats and other predators. Walls are safer than trees to some degree as cats find them difficult to climb. Try the boxes at different heights to see which species use them. Some birds, like kestrels, naturally nest at roof-top level or even higher. Make sure all boxes face north, east or south-east, to avoid strong sun and driving rain.

A RANGE OF BOXES FOR A RANGE OF BIRDS

Simple wall ledge for blackbirds, sparrows, spotted flycatchers and thrushes.

Open-fronted box for pied wagtails, robins, spotted flycatchers and wrens.

Log box for sparrows, tits and wrens.

Standard box for sparrows, tits and wrens. Hole size varies according to species: 25mm (1in) for tits, 32mm (1¼in) for sparrows.

Open-fronted box for owls and kestrels. Site as high as possible on trees or suitable buildings. Kestrels, barn owls and tawny owls have different requirements (see Barn Owl Trust or RSPB in Resources).

NOT TO SCALE

SIMPLE WALL LEDGE

OPEN-FRONTED BOX

LOG BOX

STANDARD BOX

OPEN-FRONTED OWL/KESTREL BOX

CONSTRUCTING A STANDARD NEST BOX

1. Use a plank of untreated wood 2cm (¾in) thick, 15cm (6in) wide by 1.5m (5ft) long and mark up in preparation for sawing as shown in the diagram below.

2. Saw the plank into the required pieces and make the entrance hole using a drill. The optimum hole size is 25mm for tits or 32mm for sparrows.

3. Drill two holes into the back plate, top and bottom, to enable it to be attached to the tree.

4. Nail or screw the box together, all except the lid.

5. Attach the lid to the box with a strip of leather or rubber to form a hinge and to keep out the rain. The lid can be secured at each side with small metal hooks.

FRONT

BACK

		12CM (4¾IN)	20CM (8IN)	17.5CM (7IN)	20CM (8IN)	17.5CM (7IN)	
30CM (12IN)							15CM (6IN)
BACK		BASE	ROOF	FRONT	SIDE	SIDE	

← 1.5M (5FT) →

FIXING THE BOX

Nail the box to a wooden post or tree or attach to brickwork using rawlplugs and screws. Boxes can also be hung from strong branches, using wires as shown.

AFTERCARE

Once a pair of birds has adopted the box, it should not be inspected or disturbed. Although it is tempting to keep checking on the progress of eggs and chicks, you risk frightening off the parents altogether. Instead keep a watch on the box and note down which species used it and when. Note also when the young birds leave the box, as they may return to roost there for a few weeks after leaving. In some years, a pair of birds will rear more than one brood.

In the autumn, when you are certain that the box has been vacated, you should clear out the old nesting material as this can harbour parasites.

READY-MADE NEST BOXES

Ready-made boxes and detailed plans for making a range of specialised nest boxes can be obtained from the Royal Society for the Protection of Birds (RSPB) and the British Trust for Ornithology (BTO) (see Resources).

MARCH

This is a time of great activity in the garden, as the weather softens and many species of wildlife begin their breeding cycles. In warmer areas frogs will have already laid their spawn, but in others the noisy calls of the males indicate that mating is still under way. Toads usually spawn later than frogs and newts last of all. Toad spawn is easily identifiable as the long double strands of eggs, as opposed to the frogs' clumps of jelly and the newts' eggs laid singly on pondweed. There are many threats to the developing young which may prevent them reaching maturity, but perhaps the greatest loss is the large number of adult toads killed each year by cars, as they migrate across roads to their traditional breeding ponds.

Mammals tend to be out of sight this month with fox and badger cubs being born underground. Birds are also busy building nests and defending their territories against intruders. Nesting material is drawn from a wide variety of garden sources, including grass stems, strips of bark, dead leaves and moss taken from the lawn. A slightly unkempt garden or one with a good compost heap is a richer source of nesting material than one which is clinically neat and tidy.

The onset of spring is signalled by a flush of yellow flowers. The vivid yellows of celandines, narcissus and primula seem to act as a beacon to insects emerging from hibernation to seek pollen. The true wild daffodil (*Narcissus pseudonarcissus*) may also appear this month or in early April. It is smaller and less ostentatious than its hybridised cousins and perfectly suited to the wildlife garden.

TASKS FOR THE MONTH

- ☐ Reduce bird feeding
- ☐ Weed and mulch borders
- ☐ Lift and divide water plants
- ☐ Clip heathers and lavender
- ☐ Sow half-hardy annuals under glass

BIRD FEEDING

Unless the weather is particularly harsh, reduce feeding as nesting begins. Hard bread and peanuts are harmful to newly hatched birds, so restrict food supplies to soft fat or grated cheese. Reducing the amount of food supplied will encourage the adults to start feeding on the emerging insects. However, if the ground is frozen, keep up the feeding until the bad weather passes.

DEALING WITH WEEDS

Perennial flower and shrub borders should be checked now for weeds and unwanted seedlings. Perennial weeds like ground elder will need to be dug out thoroughly as even the tiniest section of root left in the soil can sprout again. Annual weeds can be dealt with more easily, by disturbing only the top layer of soil. Use a garden fork (or hand fork) to lift them out of the soil, pulling the plant and stem cleanly away.

MULCHING

To suppress further weeds from growing, cover the soil with a layer of mulch. This can be any material that excludes light from the soil, thus preventing weeds from growing. Black polythene or old carpet will suppress weeds and conserve the moisture already in the ground, although neither looks particularly attractive. A 5–8cm (2–3in) layer of chopped bark gives a natural woodland floor finish and birds do not seem to mind scattering the pieces to find insects. Another alternative is garden compost, which has the added bonus of releasing its nutrients into the soil throughout the spring and summer. These mulches will prevent the need to use chemical weedkillers and cut down on watering later in the summer.

DIVIDING MARGINAL POND AND WETLAND PLANTS

In established ponds, marginal species can outgrow their space in the shallow water around the edge and need to be renewed by division. Spring is the best time to do this, just as the plants are starting their growth.

Dividing clump-forming plants

This applies to marsh marigold (*Caltha palustris*) and most other moisture-loving perennials.

- Marginal plants that grow in clumps or mounds can be broken up simply with a hand fork. Lift the plant out of the soil or water and, using the fork, prise away small clumps from the outside of the main clump. Choose young, healthy-looking parts of the plant and discard the interior which may have become exhausted.

- Replant the new pieces immediately, into other parts of the pond. If not needed immediately, they can be grown on in pots of wet compost.

Dividing creeping plants

This method applies to flowering rush (*Butomus umbellatus*), bog bean (*Menyanthes trifoliata*), bog arum (*Calla palustris*), water mint (*Mentha aquatica*) and lesser celandine (*Ranunculus ficaria*). The roots of these plants have a scrambling habit and can be increased by dividing the horizontal rootstock into sections.

- Remove the plant from the water and cut the rootstock into short sections. Each should have a healthy bud or young shoot and preferably a trace of roots attached.

- On flowering rush, look for a small bulb-like formation (bulbil) at the point where the leaves meet the hard woody rootstock. Make sure each section includes a bulbil. Plant these sections in trays of wet compost until they root and form healthy young plants.

CLIPPING FLOWERING HEATHER AND LAVENDER

The dead flowerheads of the summer-flowering heather (*Calluna vulgaris*) and scented lavender (*Lavandula*) can be clipped now to make way for new growth. Use a pair of garden shears and trim off the straggly dry stems, taking care not to cut into the woody parts. Both plants are valuable for bees, while heather also attracts a range of other insects and provides good cover for birds, insects and reptiles.

SOWING HALF-HARDY ANNUALS

Some of the summer garden nectar flowers are not fully hardy and need to be sown indoors this month (alternatively, buy as bedding plants in late spring). A greenhouse is not necessary to sow half-hardy annuals from seed and they can be successfully raised in the house.

- Fill 8cm (3in) pots (or seed trays) with proprietary seed compost. Water with a fine-rose watering-can; allow to drain before sowing. Firm down the compost to a flat surface.

- Sow the seed thinly on the surface, spacing it out as evenly as possible. Press larger seeds into the surface of the compost. Fine seeds do not need to be covered.

- Label pots and cover each with a small plastic bag, securing it with a rubber band or just folding it under the pot. Place in a warm place, out of direct sunlight: an airing cupboard, shaded windowsill or greenhouse propagator.

- Open the plastic bags daily to release any built-up moisture, and check for signs of germination. When the first signs of growth appear (one to three weeks), remove the bags and move pots to a lighter position – a windowsill or greenhouse bench. Water occasionally if the compost dries out.

- When three or more leaves have appeared, carefully separate the seedlings and transfer to individual pots. Leave to grow on until planting out in the garden in late spring, when the danger of frost is passed.

NECTAR FLOWERS TO SOW INDOORS

African marigold (*Tagetes erecta*)

French marigold (*Tagetes patula*)

Heliotrope (*Heliotropium*)

Petunia

Tobacco plant (*Nicotiana*)

Plants of the Month

WOOD ANEMONE
(Anemone nemorosa)

The wood anemone or 'wind flower' is a native of woodland, hedgerows and copses and makes a good, if somewhat rampant, garden plant.

TYPE Perennial, rhizomes

FLOWERS White, flushed with pink, spring

HEIGHT 15–20cm (6–8in)

PLANTING Plant rhizomes in autumn, 5cm (2in) deep and 15cm (6in) apart

SITE Sun or partial shade, under deciduous trees, hedges or in woodland clearings

SOIL Any well-drained fertile soil

CARE No special care needed

PROPAGATION Spreads rapidly by underground rhizomes. Divide rhizomes in late summer after foliage has died back

RELATED Anemone blanda, derived from a Greek wildflower, is widely grown in gardens for its blue or mauve flowers which are particularly attractive to bee flies. The yellow wood anemone (A. ranunculoides) may also be naturalised in shady areas

WILDLIFE The wood anemone relies on bees and flies for its pollination and many flying insects actively seek out the flowers when they appear in spring

CROCUS (Crocus species and hybrids)

The vast array of garden hybrid crocuses start flowering in late winter and bring some welcome colour. Easily naturalised in grass or in flower beds they will take care of themselves and give a reliable show year after year.

TYPE Bulb

FLOWERS Purple, mauve, white, yellow, late winter to mid-spring

HEIGHT 8cm (3in)

PLANTING Plant bulbs in early autumn, 8cm (3in) deep and 10cm (4in) apart

SITE Sun or shade. In grass, under trees, in beds or rockeries

SOIL Any, but prefers well drained

CARE When grown in a lawn, leave the grass uncut until the leaves have died down

PROPAGATION Lift established plants as soon as the leaves turn brown. Leave to dry, then remove the largest offsets and replant

RELATED C. tomasinianus is a purple crocus. good for growing in grass. C. chrysanthus hybrids come in every shade of yellow, making eye-catching clumps in pots or beds. The true spring crocus (C. Vemus) can be found naturalised in scattered parts of Britain although it does not flower until mid-spring

WILDLIFE A flock of sparrows can demolish a bed of crocuses in no time at all. Bees will also seek out the pollen on warm days

LESSER CELANDINE
(*Ranunculus ficaria*)

An abundant member
of the buttercup family,
the lesser celandine
is found growing wild
in woodlands and
hedgerows, by streams
and in damp hollows. It
tends to spread rapidly
in the right conditions, so should only be
planted where there is enough room for it
not to become troublesome.

TYPE Perennial, tuber

FLOWERS Bright yellow, early to late spring

HEIGHT 10cm (4in)

PLANTING Plant between early autumn
and late winter, burying the tuberous roots
5cm (2in) deep

SITE Full or partial shade, in woodlands,
ditches, hedgerows, wetlands

SOIL Any, moist

CARE No special care needed

PROPAGATION Divide and replant in mid-
autumn or early spring. Spreads very easily

WILDLIFE Relies on insects, particularly
flies and bees, for its pollination. Early
source of nectar and pollen

FLOWERING CURRANT
(*Ribes sanguineum*)

Not a native plant, but
the bees flock to the
deep pink flowers of
R. sanguineum as soon
as they open. It goes
on flowering for several
months – longer than most
other exotic garden shrubs.

TYPE Deciduous shrub

FLOWERS Deep rose-red, spring

HEIGHT 1.8–2.5m (6–8ft)

SPREAD 1.5–2.2m (5–7ft)

PLANTING Container-grown shrubs can be
planted at any time, although late autumn or
early spring gives young plants the best chance
of success

SITE Sun or light shade, shrub border

SOIL Any well-drained soil

CARE Apply a mulch of garden compost or
manure in spring. Cut out any old wood at
ground level as soon as possible after flowering

PROPAGATION By hardwood cuttings in autumn

WILDLIFE R. sanguineum is attractive to early
bees and one of the best sources of spring
nectar. Sparrows and tits also use the bush for
picking off aphids

POLLEN COUNT

*It is not only flying insects
and butterflies that are
attracted to the pollen in
spring flowers. Small mammals
like voles and woodmice will
seek out pollen as a useful
source of protein.*

MAKING A WILDLIFE POND

Probably the single most useful thing gardeners can do for wildlife is to make a pond. Even a steep-sided formal pond can be adapted to make it more friendly to wildlife (see Adapting a Formal Pond for Wildlife). The best design is a shallow contoured pool which will allow access to a range of creatures. Water is essential for frogs, toads and newts who will use it to breed. It is also useful as a drinking station for hedgehogs and foxes and as a bathing area for birds. A good range of insects specific to water and marsh habitats will use the pond, including dragonflies, damselflies, water spiders and waterboatmen. It will also become a breeding ground for midges which are an important food source for bats, swifts and swallows through the summer months.

WHERE TO SITE THE POND

Choose a sunny position, on level ground and away from overhanging trees. If the water might be a danger to young children, it should be positioned well away from the house and, if necessary, fenced off. Make use of any natural hollows in the land to reduce the amount of digging needed, although avoid those that already have water in them as further excavation would be difficult. It is a good idea to place one side of the pond adjacent to a border of low-growing shrubs or dense planting. As new frogs hatch in spring, they need cover to escape being eaten by birds. In any case, one side of the pond should be made inaccessible to human feet, to give pond wildlife an undisturbed area.

SIZE

Make the pond as large as space will allow, but at least 3m (10ft) square. With smaller ponds it is difficult to make the sides slope gently enough and it is harder to maintain a healthy balance of plants and water creatures. At some point the pond should be 75cm (2½ft) deep to prevent complete freezing in winter.

INTRODUCING FROGS AND TOADS

Don't bring in tadpoles or frogspawn from a neighbouring pond as this can risk spreading amphibian diseases and invasive plant species. The best advice is to let nature take its course. Be patient and frogs, toads and even newts will find their way to your pond. Frogs can travel up to 1km (²/₃ mile) and toads are known to travel up to 2km (1 1/4 miles) from where they were born.

CONSTRUCTING THE POND

Use a flexible butyl rubber liner. There are cheaper alternatives available, and if choosing one of these, make sure it has a guarantee of at least ten years' life. The size of the liner needed can be calculated using the following formula:

Liner width = Pond width + (2 x max pond depth) + 30cm (12in)

Liner length = Pond length + (2 x max pond depth) + 30cm (12in)

The extra 30cm (12in) is necessary to allow for an overlap all around the edge.

1. Mark out the shape of the pond using a flexible hosepipe, rope or short canes. Rounded curves look more natural than angular shapes. For a small pond, tight curves will be difficult to dig, so choose a simple oval shape. Large ponds can be lagoon, figure-of-eight or pear-shaped.

2. Remove a strip of turf (or soil), 30cm (12in) wide and 5–8cm (2–3in) deep all the way around the edge of the pond, outside the shape marked. Lay the turves aside for later use. Start to dig the pond within the marked area, starting from the outside and working in. Remove turf, soil and stones, making a series of shelves and gentle slopes. For marginal plants, a shelf at about 23cm (9in) deep is useful.

3. When the contouring of the soil inside the pond is complete, pat down the soil and remove any sharp stones. Lay a plank of wood across the pond (widthways and lengthways) and, using a spirit level, make a final check that the sides are level.

4. Put a 5–8cm (2–3in) layer of damp builders' sand over the soil to give extra protection to the liner. Pat the sand down firmly to the contours of the pond. Old carpet, carpet underlay or sheets of wet cardboard can be used instead.

5. Unfold the liner over the hole and ease it into position. Anchor the outside edge using stones. A pile of smooth stones can also be put at the deepest part to hold the liner in position and may be left in place after the pool is filled.

6. Over the butyl liner, put another protective layer, such as matting (sold in garden centres as an underlayer), plus a layer of poor garden soil (riddled to get rid of stones) or a sand-and-gravel mixture. This serves two functions, as a protection for the liner and as a rooting medium for the plants. Don't use compost or rich soil which contains too many nutrients. Fill the pond, using tap water via a hose. As the pond fills up, ease off the edges of the liner as necessary by removing the stones.

7. Trim off any excess liner, and finish the pond by laying turf or paving stones over the 30cm (12in) strip around the edge.

PLANTING THE POND

Leave the water to settle for a week or two before beginning planting. Early spring is a good time to start planting, but in fact plants can be put in right through the summer and into early autumn. The aim is to include as many native species as possible and to select a range of plants with different habits of growth (see Plants for the Pond). Oxygenating plants grow underwater and help to keep the water clean. They also support an incredible variety of microscopic creatures and provide food for water snails. Aquatic plants with floating leaves, like water lilies, shade parts of the water from the sun, which in turn controls algae growth. The leaves are also used as convenient stepping stones for amphibians and small birds. Marginal plants thrive in shallow water at the edges of the pond and form the link between the pond and the rest of the garden. These plants, with most of their stems, leaves and flowers out of the water, provide cover for young frogs and toads. The taller species are particularly important for dragonflies, who lay their eggs on the stems.

ATTRACTING WILDLIFE TO THE POND

Many water creatures will be introduced to the pond when the plants are put in, including water snails who lay their eggs on the underside of large-leaved plants like lilies. Many flying insects will colonise the water without being introduced, particularly pond skaters and dragonflies. It is not advisable to bring in mud, water, frog spawn or tadpoles from other ponds as this can spread disease and invasive plants. Creatures wil make their way to a healthy pond as it gets established.

POND MANAGEMENT

The best pond management system is to leave it alone as much as possible. Ponds take time to reach an equilibrium and attempts to speed this up by using chemicals to clear the water will result in a serious imbalance. The most frequent pond problem is the build-up of algae and pondweed. Both are usually kept under control by a healthy population of native water snails. Too much algae is also an indicator that the water is too rich in nutrients. To counteract this, top up the pond with rainwater instead of tapwater and never add compost or garden soil which contains fertilisers. Another way of reducing the build-up of nutrients is to remove some of the vegetation in late summer or early autumn.

LINKING A MARSH OR WETLAND AREA TO THE POND

It is possible to incorporate a marshy area linked to the main pond. When excavating the pond, an additional shallow area is dug, divided from the rest of the pond by a line of heavy stones. The area is backfilled with soil and as the water level in the pond rises, water percolates into the marsh area and drains back into the pond.

In practice, this can be a rather tricky feature to get right, and in many ponds the earth tends to be drawn back into the pond or, conversely, the water is sucked out of the pond and into the marsh. It might be better to make an independent wetland garden (see the practical project for April).

ADAPTING A FORMAL POND FOR WILDLIFE

Formal ponds can be adapted to the needs of wildlife without the need to build a whole new structure.

- Phase out ornamental fish, as these will eat tadpoles otherwise.

- Add 'steps' to counteract the steep sides and make it easier for birds, amphibians and small mammals to get access to shallow water. A series of bricks or large rocks can form a link between the deepest part of the pool and the edge of the pond.

- Soften the edges of the pond with marginal planting to provide cover for frogs and toads. Prop planting baskets on bricks if the water is too deep.

- Introduce more native species, gradually replacing exotic plants with their native equivalents, to increase the range of insects using the plants for breeding and feeding.

WATER LILY CHOICES

For small ponds, the fringed water lily is a better choice than the gigantic white lily which can cover the entire water surface.

WARNING

Avoid Canadian pondweed (Elodea canadensis) – although commonly sold in garden centres it tends to swamp all other vegetation and is difficult to control.

MARGINAL PLANTS

BRICKS

PLANTS FOR THE POND

NATIVE OXYGENATORS

Curled pondweed (*Potamogeton crispus*)

Hornwort (*Ceratophyllum demersum*)

Spiked water milfoil
(*Myriophyllum spicatum*)

Water starwort (*Callitriche stagnalis*)

HABIT Fully submerged, although flowers
often appear just above the surface.

PLANTING Plant bunches in soil in deepest
part of the pond. Anchor with bricks
or rock until established. Oxygenators
increase rapidly so introduce only a few
bunches at first – as a guide, allow four to
five bunches for a 3m (10ft) square pond.

NATIVE FLOATING-LEAVED PLANTS

Amphibious bistort
(*Polygonum amphibium*)

Common water crowfoot
(*Ranunculus aquatilis*)

Fringed water lily (*Nymphoides peltata*)

Frogbit (*Hydrocharis morus-ranae*)

White water lily (*Nymphaea alba*)

HABIT Root at the bottom, but leaves and
flowers float on the surface of the water.

PLANTING Anchor individual plants in soil
with heavy stones until well established.

NATIVE MARGINALS

Bog bean (*Menyanthes
trifoliata*) PD = 15–45cm (6–18in)

Flowering rush (*Butomus umbellatus*)
PD = 8–15cm (3–6in)

Lesser reedmace (*Typha angustifolia*)
W, PD = 8–15cm (3–6in) or wet soil

Lesser spearwort (*Ranunculus flammula*)
W, PD = 8–15cm (3–6in) or wet soil

Marsh marigold (*Caltha palustris*)
W, PD = 0–8cm (0–3in) or wet soil

Water mint (*Mentha aquatica*)
W, PD = 0–8cm (0–3in) or wet soil

Yellow flag iris (*Iris pseudacorus*)
PD = 0–15cm (0–6in)

HABIT Grow in shallow water towards the
edges of the pond, with most of the stem,
leaves and flowers above water.

PLANTING Plant directly into the soil on
shelves or gentle slopes within the optimum
depth range.

KEY

PD = Planting depth, the depth of water
above the soil level

W = Indicates these plants will grow in
shallow water or wet soil and are suitable
for the wetland garden too (see the
practical project for April)

AVOID OVERPLANTING

*Don't be tempted to cram too many plants into a small water
area. A balanced pool needs areas of open water, as well as margins
of dense planting.*

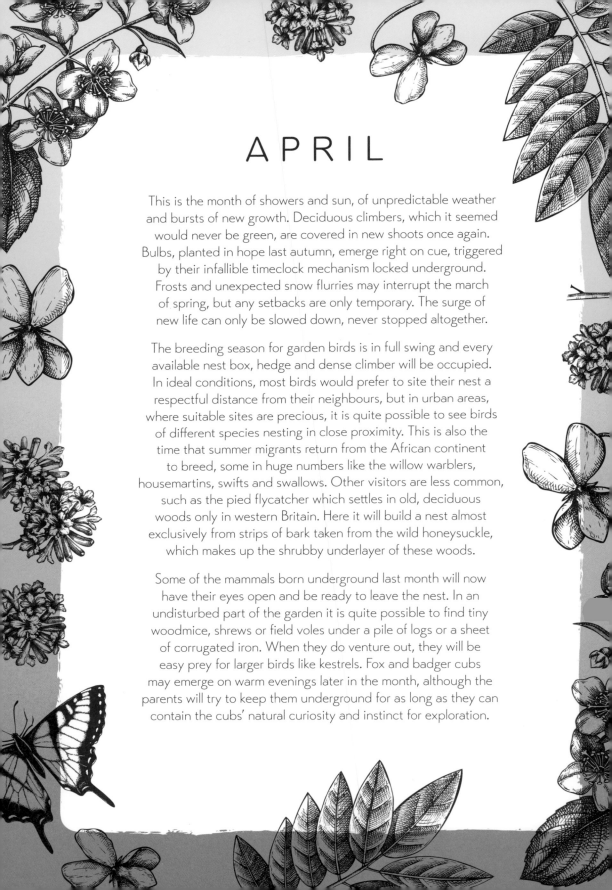

APRIL

This is the month of showers and sun, of unpredictable weather and bursts of new growth. Deciduous climbers, which it seemed would never be green, are covered in new shoots once again. Bulbs, planted in hope last autumn, emerge right on cue, triggered by their infallible timeclock mechanism locked underground. Frosts and unexpected snow flurries may interrupt the march of spring, but any setbacks are only temporary. The surge of new life can only be slowed down, never stopped altogether.

The breeding season for garden birds is in full swing and every available nest box, hedge and dense climber will be occupied. In ideal conditions, most birds would prefer to site their nest a respectful distance from their neighbours, but in urban areas, where suitable sites are precious, it is quite possible to see birds of different species nesting in close proximity. This is also the time that summer migrants return from the African continent to breed, some in huge numbers like the willow warblers, housemartins, swifts and swallows. Other visitors are less common, such as the pied flycatcher which settles in old, deciduous woods only in western Britain. Here it will build a nest almost exclusively from strips of bark taken from the wild honeysuckle, which makes up the shrubby underlayer of these woods.

Some of the mammals born underground last month will now have their eyes open and be ready to leave the nest. In an undisturbed part of the garden it is quite possible to find tiny woodmice, shrews or field voles under a pile of logs or a sheet of corrugated iron. When they do venture out, they will be easy prey for larger birds like kestrels. Fox and badger cubs may emerge on warm evenings later in the month, although the parents will try to keep them underground for as long as they can contain the cubs' natural curiosity and instinct for exploration.

TASKS FOR THE MONTH

☐ Put away the bird table

☐ Sow hardy annual seeds outdoors

☐ First cut of new flowering meadow

☐ Plant pond and wetland plants

☐ Plant climbers and put up trellis

BIRD TABLE STORAGE

The bird table can be put away now and stored for next winter. Wash down the surfaces with a mild disinfectant and water to remove all traces of food and droppings.

SOW HARDY ANNUAL SEEDS

As the weather improves, many annual garden and wildflowers can be sown from seed outdoors. This is one of the cheapest and easiest ways to provide flowering nectar plants for the garden's insects and is ideal for anyone starting a garden from scratch. By choosing hardy species that won't be harmed by any unexpectedly cold weather, the seeds can be sown directly into the ground where they are intended to grow and do not need to be nursed in greenhouses or coldframes.

- Prepare the soil by lightly forking over, removing any large stones or clods of earth. Water thoroughly.

- Sprinkle the seeds by hand over the whole area. Rake in the seeds to make sure they are just buried.

- If there is no rain for a day or two after sowing, water the ground with a fine-rose watering-can, making sure the water soaks deeply into the soil.

Aftercare

Remove any competing weed seedlings as they come up between the flowers. When they only have two or three pairs of leaves it is difficult to tell the difference, so wait until the plants are easily recognisable. Thin out any groups of plants that are overcrowded, by removing some of the seedlings. Continue to water annual beds throughout the summer, particularly during hot, dry spells.

CUTTING THE NEW FLOWERING MEADOW

New wildflower lawns or meadows, sown the previous autumn, should have their first cut when the grass reaches a height of 10cm (4in) (see the practical project for September). This is only applicable to lawns sown with a standard grass and perennial flower mixture and not those containing annual flowers which are cut in late summer.

Before mowing, roll the lawn lightly to make sure the seedlings are securely bedded in the soil. Use a heavy-duty rotary mower or motor-scythe, and cut at a height of 5–8cm (2–3in). (These machines can be hired by the day from local tool-hire shops.) A sharp hand scythe also cuts the grass efficiently, but should only be handled by people trained in its use. Leave the cuttings in place for a day or two to allow any creatures to crawl back into the meadow, then rake off and add to the compost heap.

PLANTING WATER AND WETLAND PLANTS

Spring is a good time to put in container-grown pond plants, although they can be planted at any time between now and late autumn. Select a place in the pond with the right depth of water, according to the growing preferences of the plant (see March for plant lists). Gently insert the roots into the soil or growing medium in the pond. Place a small stone on top of the root ball to secure the plant until the roots start to anchor themselves. At this time of year growth is rapid and new plants should establish easily.

KEEP YOUR DISTANCE

Don't be tempted to get too close to nesting birds this month in an attempt to see when the young are hatched. Keep disturbance to a minimum by observing the parents' movements from a safe distance, using binoculars to get a better view of the nest or box.

RECOMMENDED HARDY ANNUALS

Candytuft (*Iberis umbellata*) N

Clarkia (*Clarkia elegans*) B, C

California poppy (*Eschscholzia californica*) N, B, H

Corncockle (*Agrostemma githago*) Nat, N, Po

Corn chamomile (*Anthemis arvensis*) Nat, N

Cornflower (*Centaurea cyanus*) Nat, N, B

Larkspur (*Delphinium consolida*) Nat, B, Po

Love-in-a-mist (*Nigella damascena*) N, B

Mignonette (*Reseda odorata*) N

Nasturtium (*Tropaeolum majus*) C, H

Night-scented stock (*Matthiola bicornis*) N, M

Poached egg flower (*Limnanthes douglasii*) B, H, N

Pot marigold (*Calendula officinalis*) B, H, N

Sunflower (*Helianthus annuus*) N, B, S

Virginia stock (*Malcolmia maritima*) N

PLANTING CLIMBERS

Spring is a good time to put in new climbers, giving them a chance of making enough growth to cover a wall or fence by the end of the season. For wildlife, the main consideration is to ensure that there is a gap between the flat surface and the climber itself, making a secluded enclave for nesting or roosting. The usual framework for non-clinging plants (i.e., everything except ivy and creepers) is a wooden trellis or horizontal wires. Instead of nailing the trellis flat against the wall, small wooden battens are screwed to the wall first, to hold the trellis several centimetres (a few inches) away. Similarly, the 'eyes' which hold the wires can be attached to the battens rather than being put straight into the wall.

Planting container-grown climbers

· Water the plant well in its pot. Carefully detach the top growth from its support, removing wires, ties or canes.

· Dig a hole 30cm (12in) away from the wall. It should be as deep as and slightly wider than the container. (The plant should sit in the hole so that the surface of the compost is level with the surrounding soil.)

· Mix a little garden compost or well-rotted manure with the soil taken from the hole and add a spadeful to the bottom of the hole. Remove the plant from its container and place in the hole.

· Fill around the roots with the soil mixture, treading down firmly. Water thoroughly, making sure the water soaks right down around the roots.

RECOMMENDED CLIMBING PLANTS

Ceanothus (C. x burkwoodii) N, E
Aspect – south, west

Cotoneaster (C. horizontalis) B, F
Aspect – north, east

Firethorn (Pyracantha) N, F, E
Aspect – north, east

Honeysuckle (Lonicera periclymenum) Nat, N, B
Bark for nests
Aspect – east, west

Ivy (Hedera helix) Nat, N, B, C, F
Aspect – north, east, west

Old man's beard (Clematis vitalba) Nat, N
Any aspect

Summer Jasmine (Jasminum officinialis)
Aspect - south N, B

All these climbers may be used as nesting sites for birds and possibly for bat roosts as well.

PLANTING TIMES

Container-grown climbers can be planted at any time of the year, although it is best to avoid mid-summer and mid-winter.

Plants of the Month

ENGLISH BLUEBELL
(Scilla non-scripta)

The native bluebell is found growing in open woodlands, on grass banks and heaths. The old coppiced woodlands which suited it so well are declining and so natural colonies are becoming rare, but as a garden flower it is not difficult to establish.

TYPE Perennial bulb

FLOWERS Violet-blue (occasionally white or pink), mid-spring to early summer

HEIGHT 30cm (12in)

PLANTING Plant bulbs in groups in early autumn, 10–15cm (4–6in) deep and 15cm (6in) apart. Bulbs do not store well, so plant as soon as possible after purchase

SITE Sun or partial shade. Bluebells prefer some shade from the summer sun, under deciduous trees, or hedges

SOIL Moist, with plenty of organic matter. Will tolerate drier conditions

CARE Leave undisturbed if possible

PROPAGATION Bluebells self-seed easily, but can also be increased by division. Lift clumps after leaves have died down, divide the bulbs and replant the offsets immediately

RELATED The Spanish bluebell (S. hispanica) has escaped and become naturalised in Britain. The flowers are more erect and are available in a wider range of colours

WILDLIFE Many early insects will visit the bluebell for nectar, but its real value in the wildlife garden is for conservation of an irreplaceable wild plant

WILD DAFFODIL
(Narcissus pseudonarcissus)

Also known as the Lent lily, the wild daffodil is smaller and less conspicuous than its garden counterparts. Its natural habitat is meadows and deciduous woodlands, where it carpets the ground in drifts. In the garden it may be naturalised in grass and under trees.

TYPE Bulb, perennial

FLOWERS Cream to pale yellow, mid-spring

HEIGHT 15–30cm (6–12in)

PLANTING Plant bulbs in autumn, 8cm (3in) deep

SITE In sun or partial shade, under deciduous trees or hedges, or in grass

SOIL Any ordinary garden soil

CARE Prefers to be undisturbed. Clumps which become overcrowded or flower poorly may need to be lifted and divided

PROPAGATION Divide bulbs only after they have been growing in situ for several years. Lift clumps in early summer, remove healthy offsets and replant immediately

WILDLIFE N. pseudonarcissus is becoming less widespread in the wild, as more cultivated varieties escape (or are planted) on road verges and open spaces. Naturalised colonies in gardens may ensure its future survival

SNAKESHEAD FRITILLARY
(*Fritillaria meleagris*)

This delicate spring flower grows naturally in the damp water meadows of southern Britain but is now very rare in the wild. It has been grown in gardens for many centuries, and makes a pretty addition to a spring-flowering meadow, grassy area or border.

TYPE Perennial bulb

FLOWERS Pink or purple with chequered markings or white with green markings, mid- to late spring

HEIGHT 30cm (12in)

PLANTING Plant bulbs as soon as possible after purchase, in autumn. Handle carefully as they are prone to bruising. Place them 10–15cm (4–6in) deep and 15cm (6in) apart

SITE Sun or light shade. In borders, meadows, or grassy areas

SOIL Moist, fertile soil

CARE Leave undisturbed for at least four years. Lift and divide in early summer, after leaves have died down

PROPAGATION Once well established, snakeshead fritillary will self-seed. It can also be increased by division. Lift bulbs in early summer, remove the offsets and replant immediately

WILDLIFE A useful addition to the spring meadow, providing nectar for early butterflies and insects. Like the bluebell, it is one of the most beautiful threatened wildflowers and deserves to be grown for that reason alone

COMMON GRAPE HYACINTH
(*Muscari neglectum*)

A rare wildflower in Britain, the grape hyacinth is increasingly grown in cultivation. Its natural habitat is dry grassland and it adapts well to several garden situations.

TYPE Perennial bulb

FLOWERS Deep blue and tipped with white, spring

HEIGHT 20cm (8in)

PLANTING Plant bulbs in groups in early autumn. Place them 8cm (3in) deep and 10cm (4in) apart

SITE Open, sunny site; grass, beds or pots

SOIL Any

CARE No special care needed. Clumps which are not flowering well should be lifted and divided after leaves have died back in early summer

PROPAGATION Grape hyacinth self-seeds very readily and clumps should spread without intervention. Bulbs can also be divided and replanted in early summer

RELATED Commonly grown garden species include the small, sky-blue *M. botryoides*. At only 15cm (6in) tall it is useful for rock gardens and for planting along the edges of paths

WILDLIFE The strong blue colour attracts a wide range of butterflies, including tortoiseshells, brimstones and peacocks, who feed on the nectar

COWSLIP (Primula veris)

One of the prettiest spring-flowering natives, the cowslip is an inhabitant of meadows and pastures. It is difficult to find in the wild, due to overpicking and to modern agricultural practices, but has become a popular garden plant.

TYPE Perennial

FLOWERS Deep yellow, orange markings in the centre, mid- to late spring

HEIGHT 15–23cm (6–9in)

PLANTING Plant pot-grown specimens in autumn or early spring. Set the plants 23–30cm (9–12in) apart

SITE Sun or partial shade, in spring-flowering meadows, grassy banks or borders

SOIL Any, but dislikes acid soils

CARE No special care needed

PROPAGATION By division immediately after flowering or by seed collected in early summer and sown fresh. Cowslip seeds may take several years to germinate

WILDLIFE An important component of the spring-flowering meadow. A vital early source of nectar for insects, particularly the spring brood of white butterflies, it is also a caterpillar food plant for the Duke of Burgundy fritillary which lays its eggs on the plant in late spring

OXLIP (Primula elatior)

The oxlip is so closely related to the cowslip that it was not recognised as a separate species until the last century. The flowers of the oxlip are a paler yellow and do not have the orange markings. In the wild, it is most easily found in ancient coppiced woods in the east of England. It prefers a damper, shadier habitat than the cowslip and can be happily grown amongst coppiced trees, on the banks of a stream, or in a wetland habitat. Oxlips rely on early bees and butterflies for pollination.

NATIVE SPRING BULBS

Common grape hyacinth (*Muscari neglectum*)

English bluebell (*Scilla non-scripta*)

Ramsons garlic (*Allium ursinum*)

Snakeshead fritillary (*Fritillaria meleagris*)

Wild daffodil (*Narcissus pseudonarcissus*)

Spring crocus (*Crocus vernus*)

MAKING AND PLANTING A WETLAND

Undoubtedly one of the most fragile natural environments, wetlands are under threat from development in many areas of the country, indeed the world. This applies as much to the flood plains and water meadows bordering inconspicuous streams and rivers as it does to the major coastal estuaries. Even within our largest cities, small areas of wetland or marsh still exist and need to be identified and protected. They may be home to some spectacular wildlife – short-eared owls, for example – and also some very ordinary plants like reedmace, sedge and meadowsweet, which are no less interesting for being commonplace. An area of wetland or marsh extends the range of habitats available to wildlife in the garden. Many plants prefer a waterlogged soil rather than shallow water and they include some of our prettiest native flowers. Species like ragged robin are becoming increasingly rare in the wild and rely on garden cultivation for their future survival. Wetlands have their own balance of plants and creatures which is related though different to the pool habitat. It is quite possible to make a wetland area whether or not the garden already has a pond. For families with young children, a marshy area, might be a safer alternative to even the shallowest pool. The marsh can be attached to the pond (see March) or completely separate, even in a different part of the garden.

MARSH WETLAND WILDLIFE

Orange tip butterflies

Frogs and toads

Bats

Swifts, swallows and housemartins

Slow worms

Bees

Hoverflies

MAKING AN INDEPENDENT MARSH AREA

A natural wetland would draw its water from two sources: from above (rainwater) and from below, drawing from the underground water table. In the garden wetland, the liner is designed to retain most of the topwater and little will be drawn up from below. However, it is important to have some filtering of water through the marsh if it is not to become sour and waterlogged. Short lengths of hosepipe can be inserted through the liner into the ground below to take water out, but a few drainage holes in the bottom of the liner will do the job almost as well.

1. Choose an area of level ground, away from overhanging trees and avoiding the main routes through the garden.

2. Dig a hollow, with gently sloping sides to a depth of between 45–60cm (18–24in). Do not make it any shallower than this as the soil will dry out too quickly in hot weather. Make a shelf around the edge, 15cm (6in) wide and 5–8cm (2–3in) deep. Remove any sharp stones.

3. Line the hollow with a flexible liner, allowing a 15cm (6in) overlap around the edge. The liner does not have to be butyl as it will be protected from sunlight by the soil – heavy duty polythene or a cheaper proprietary liner will be adequate. Secure the liner around the edge with a few heavy stones. Make a few drainage holes in the deepest part of the hollow.

4. Fill the hollow with any good, water-retentive soil. Usually the soil that has been excavated can be used, provided it has not been treated with chemicals. If it is particularly sandy, mix it with well-rotted garden compost or leaf mould. Alternatively, use a proprietary loam-based compost for filling.

5. Remove the anchoring stones and disguise the overlapping edge of the liner with a row of tiles, bricks or turf. Alternatively, simply cover the overlap with more soil; in time the plants will spill out from the bed and the edge will no longer be visible.

6. Wet the marsh thoroughly after construction with a hosepipe or watering-can.

PEAT BOGS

An altogether different habitat to the wetland or marsh is the peat bog, found in isolated pockets of Scotland, Wales and upland England. Peat bogs are fed by rainwater (rather than groundwater or the overflow of streams) and occur on poorly drained land. Their identifying characteristic is the sphagnum mosses which grow and decay eventually to form layers of peat. Draining these bogs to extract the peat has been one of the major threats to their continued existence. Finding alternatives to peat in the garden (such as homemade compost, leaf-mould and peat substitutes) is one of the main ways gardeners can help to safeguard natural peat bogs.

PLANTING UP THE MARSH

Once the marsh is completed you can start to add suitable plants. New plants should be watered in their pots before planting. Remove from their pots and, using a trowel, insert them into the damp soil, pressing them in firmly. Remember that marsh plants spread very quickly once they are established, so leave enough room for them to grow to their full size. In a small marsh it is best to leave out lady's smock, which can become invasive.

If the marsh is attached to the pond, it looks better if smaller plants are put nearest the pond, graduating the heights so that the tallest of the marsh plants are furthest away from the water. However, if the marsh is an 'island', it can be designed to be viewed from all directions. Plant tall-growing meadowsweet and hemp agrimony in the centre of the bed, using creeping plants like marsh St John's wort to spill out and disguise the edges.

The established wetland will provide a valuable additional wildlife habitat.

MAINTAINING THE WETLAND

In most areas, the rainfall will be sufficient to keep the soil consistently wet. However, in times of drought, or in particularly dry areas, additional watering will be necessary. The best way to water a wetland is to allow water to trickle in gradually, either through a purpose-designed trickle irrigation system or by connecting a hosepipe to an outside tap, turned on just enough to allow water to drip out. If neither method is available, check the bed regularly and top up with a watering-can as needed. As with a pond (see March), plant foliage should be cut back in early autumn to prevent too many dead leaves clogging up the marsh. Plants which have overgrown their space can be lifted in early autumn.

WETLAND WILDLIFE

Many of the creatures attracted to a pond will also use the wetland. Frogs and toads may well spend the winter hibernating in the mud, only returning to the water to breed in the spring. Slow worms are particularly useful wetland visitors, eating large quantities of slugs and caterpillars as they nestle in the damp earth.

The flowers themselves attract pollen-eating insects, which in turn are a food source for bats and summer migrant birds like swifts and swallows and housemartins. Bees and butterflies seeking nectar will also frequent the marsh flowers. Elephant hawkmoths feed on the bogbean (*Menyanthes trifoliata*) and long-tongued hoverflies search for pollen in the flowers of lady's smock (*Cardamine pratensis*). Lady's smock is also an important food plant for the caterpillars of orange tip butterflies.

Marsh betony (*Stachys palustris*) relies on bees for its pollination, and the heavy scent of meadowsweet (*Filipendula ulmaria*) is attractive to flies.

GROWING MARSH PLANTS IN CONTAINERS

Where space is limited, or simply as an alternative to conventional patio plants, it is possible to grow moisture-loving species in pots and tubs. The container needs to retain water – a terracotta pot which has a porous structure would not be suitable, but a glazed ceramic pot would work well. Plastic pots can also be used. Choose a pot at least 30cm (12in) deep and 40cm (16in) across. The best way to ensure the compost stays wet is to stand the whole pot in a substantial tray of water, so that the marsh can draw up moisture as it is needed. Ordinary plant saucers will not hold enough water, and something deeper like a large kitchen roasting tin, which may not look so elegant, will do the job more effectively.

Spring is an ideal time to plant moisture-loving plants. Fill the container with a loam-based potting compost, insert the plants and water until soaked. Choose plants that won't outgrow the limited space too quickly. Include a selection of tall-growing species like purple loosestrife (*Lythrum salicaria*), sweet flag (*Acorus calamus*) and ragged robin (*Lychnis flos-cuculi*) alongside smaller plants like bogbean (*Menyanthes trifoliata*) and oxlips (*Primula elatior*). Avoid lady's smock (*Cardamine pratensis*) and water mint (*Mentha aquatica*) which can spread too quickly. Keep the water in the base tray topped up, using rainwater collected in a water butt where possible. Keeping the tray full of water is particularly important in long, hot, dry spells, although in spring and autumn the natural rainfall will probably be adequate. Cut back the foliage in the autumn to prevent the pots becoming choked with decaying material. Repot the plants every two or three years when they start to outgrow their containers. In the second year after planting, the plants may have used up the nutrients in the compost and will need an extra boost from a slow-release fertiliser.

MOISTURE-LOVING NATIVE PLANTS

PLANT	HEIGHT	COLOUR	FLOWERING TIME
BOG BEAN (*Menyanthes trifoliata*) M	25cm (10in)	White	Mid-summer
GLOBE FLOWER (*Trollius europaeus*)	60cm (24in)	Yellow	Early summer
OXLIP (*Primula elatior*) B, N	15cm (6in)	Pale yellow	Late spring
PRIMROSE (*Primula vulgaris*) N	10cm (4in)	Pale yellow	Mid-spring
PURPLE LOOSESTRIFE (*Lythrum salicaria*) B, N	1m (3ft)	Pink-purple	Summer
RAGGED ROBIN (*Lychnis flos-cuculi*) N	60cm (24in)	Pink	Summer
SWEET FLAG (*Acorus calamus*)	60cm (24in)	Green	Mid-summer
BOG ARUM* (*Calla palustris*)	15cm (6in)	Yellow-green	Summer
HEMP AGRIMONY (*Eupatorium cannabinum*) B, N	1.2m (4ft)	Reddish-pink	Late summer
LADY'S SMOCK (*Cardamine pratensis*) H, C, N	23cm (9in)	Pale pink	Spring
MARSH BETONY (*Stachys palustris*) B	30cm (12in)	Purple	Summer
MARSH CINQUEFOIL (*Potentilla palustris*)	23cm (9in)	Dark red	Summer
MARSH ST JOHN'S WORT (*Hypericum elodes*)	15cm (6in)	Pale yellow	Summer
MEADOWSWEET (*Filipendula ulmaria*)	1m (3ft)	Creamy-white	Summer

*Naturalised in places in Britain

PLANTING TIMES

Spring is the best planting time for moisture-loving plants, but container-grown specimens will be available through to autumn from specialist nurseries.

MAY

The coming of the hawthorn blossom is one of the most reliable signs of spring. Lanes and hedgerows are filled with the distinctive scent and this is a good time to consider which native shrubs and trees could be used in the garden. Wild cherry is another tree at its best this month, the blossom swarming with insects as they forage from flower to flower in search of nectar and pollen.

Visiting old woodlands can be a source of inspiration for the wildlife gardener. Carpets of bluebells still exist in traditionally managed sites, where trampling by hoards of visitors is kept to a minimum. The cycle of coppicing trees in winter to regrow during the summer suits the bluebell perfectly. The woodland is opened up to the sunlight while the foliage and flowers are forming, but reverts to shade during the hotter summer months. Bluebells are very resistant to change and in some areas the plants persist, despite the fact that the original woodland has disappeared. In towns, evidence of lost bluebell woods may surface in street names like 'Endymion', or perhaps in the memories of the oldest residents.

Two garden 'friends' are worth observing this month. Hedgehogs are particularly active, finding partners for mating, and feeding voraciously at night. Unfortunately many hedgehogs are killed due to lack of forethought on the gardeners' part, either by getting caught in badly placed netting, eating slugs which have been poisoned by pellets, or by drowning in steep-sided ponds. Another useful garden inhabitant is the lacewing which lays its eggs on a variety of plant leaves. The brown larvae that hatch out feed greedily on aphids and small caterpillars, to grow into delicate green-coloured adults.

TASKS FOR THE MONTH

- ☐ *Plant out half-hardy annuals*
- ☐ *Clear spring borders*
- ☐ *Lift and divide primroses*
- ☐ *Prune flowering currant bushes*
- ☐ *Plant for summer and autumn*
- ☐ *Plant hanging baskets*

MAY

PLANTING OUT HALF-HARDY ANNUALS

In most areas, it will be safe to plant out half-hardy annuals like *Nicotiana* after the danger of frost is past. These may have been raised from seed indoors or in a greenhouse (see tasks for the month of March) or they can be bought this month from garden centres and markets as bedding plants. Although growing half-hardy species involves more work than perennials and hardy annuals, they will provide an extra source of pollen and nectar throughout the summer.

Preparation

Use small plants or seedlings to fill up gaps in existing beds, or to plant up containers and hanging baskets. Garden beds should be prepared by forking over the top 15–20cm (6–8in) to break up the soil to a fine texture. Fill containers with proprietary potting compost. The soil or compost should be moist before planting, so water thoroughly the day before planting if necessary. All half-hardy annuals prefer an open, sunny position.

Planting

- Separate each plant, making sure that there is a healthy root system.

- Space the plants about half their eventual height apart. Make planting holes with a trowel and firm each plant into place.

Watering

Watering should not be necessary, unless there are prolonged periods without rain.

CLEAR SPRING BORDERS

Borders or pots containing spring-flowering biennials (like wallflowers and forget-me-nots which will be reaching the end of their flowering period) can be cleared to make room for sowing hardy annual seeds (see April) or for half-hardy bedding plants. This will ensure there is a good range of nectar-producing plants in flower throughout the summer. Pull up the biennials and add to the compost heap. Fork over the soil, ready for replanting.

AVOID PLANTING IN THE HEAT
If the weather is warm, do planting in the late afternoon or evening to prevent plants from wilting in the heat.

51

LIFT AND DIVIDE PRIMROSES

Wild primroses (*Primula vulgaris*) and any garden primroses or polyanthus can be divided this month, after flowering has finished. This is a simple way of thinning out overcrowded clumps and increasing the number of plants available.

- Ease the clumps gently out of the ground with a hand fork, taking care not to tear the roots.

- Select pieces with a few roots attached and pull apart by hand. Pot them up into moist potting compost and place the pots in a shady corner of the garden.

- Keep moist throughout summer and plant out into their permanent positions early autumn.

PRUNING FLOWERING CURRANT

Flowering currant shrubs (*Ribes*) may be pruned if the plant has become too large.

- Wait until flowering has finished. Cut out the old, woody stems near the base of the plant, making the cut just above a new bud.

- Removing most of the old wood will thin out the plant considerably. Young stems should then be shortened by about a third, making the cut at the junction with a strong shoot lower down.

PLANTING FOR SUMMER AND AUTUMN

Buying bulbs and pot-grown plants means you can stock up the garden, even if you have grown nothing from seed. Garden alliums are available to buy in flower and if planted in a border or pot will go on to flower again next year. Autumn-flowering cyclamen tubers (*Cyclamen hederifolium*) can also be planted for flowering in late summer and autumn.

HALF-HARDY ANNUALS

African marigolds (*Tagetes erecta*) N, B

French marigolds (*Tagetes patula*) N, B

Heliotrope (*Heliotropium*) N, B

Petunia N

Snapdragon (*Antirrhinum*) B (hardy, but often grown as bedding)

Tobacco plant (*Nicotiana*) N

PLANTING HANGING BASKETS

Provide instant nectar for the summer months by planting up a hanging basket. Half-hardy and hardy annuals are widely available in garden centres – choose from varieties like alyssum or nasturtiums, mixed with upright French marigolds, petunias or snapdragons.

- Use a solid plastic or terracotta hanging basket. Cover the base with a 5cm (2in) layer of coarse grit. Add 8cm (3in) of potting compost.

- Arrange the plants so that the trailing varieties are at the edge and the upright ones are in the centre. Fill around the plants with more compost until it sits just below the rim of the hanging basket. Firm the plants in well and water thoroughly.

Alternative hanging basket

Instead of the traditional flowers, plant up a basket of herbs. Even a simple combination of mint and chives will attract bees, butterflies and moths. For visual effect, use several different types of mint, including the variegated varieties. Allow the chives and mints to flower for maximum wildlife value.

Plants of the Month

RAMSONS/WILD GARLIC
(Allium ursinum)

A native bulb of hedgerows, coppiced woods and shady banks, ramsons is increasingly available from wildflower nurseries. It is one of the most common members of the onion family and the leaves give off a powerful garlic smell when crushed.

TYPE Bulb

FLOWERS White, mid-spring to early summer

HEIGHT 40cm (16in)

PLANTING Plant bulbs in early autumn at twice their own depth

SITE Partial shade, in a coppiced wood, under deciduous trees or hedges

SOIL Moist

CARE Once established, clumps may be divided after flowering to produce more plants

PROPAGATION Lift and divide bulbs in summer (after flowering), replanting the offsets and small bulbs immediately; also self-seeds very readily

RELATED Most of the ornamental onions (alliums) are good for bees and butterflies, with their large pom-pom flowers – in particular, *A. sphaerocephalon*, *A. giganteum* and *A. aflatunense*

WILDLIFE Although not rare in the wild, ramsons is a good plant to grow alongside more precious woodland flowers such as bluebells. Attractive to butterflies, wasps and flying insects

BROOM (*Cytisus scoparius*)

A common native shrub of dry, sunny habitats, broom was traditionally grown for its bark, used in the tanning industry and for making ropes. The long-lasting golden yellow flowers make it a useful plant for the wildlife garden.

TYPE Deciduous shrub

FLOWERS Yellow, late spring/early summer

HEIGHT 2.5m (8ft)

SPREAD 2.5m (8ft)

PLANTING Plant container-grown specimens in autumn or early spring

SITE Full sun, shrub border

SOIL Any, well-drained

CARE Prune each year to prevent shrub becoming bare and leggy. In mid-summer, cut back only the stems that have just flowered. Take care not to cut into old wood as this will stop any new growth. Brooms tend to be short-lived and old bushes do not respond to pruning, so should be discarded after six or seven years

PROPAGATION Take hardwood cuttings in late summer

RELATED *C.* x *praecox* is a more compact bush for the smaller garden, growing to 1.5m (5ft). It flowers a month earlier

WILDLIFE The yellow flowers last for up to two months and are excellent pollen providers for bees

LILY OF THE VALLEY
(*Convallaria majalis*)

A relatively rare native plant of woodlands and meadows. It is widely grown in gardens for its sweet scent and nodding bell-like flowers, but needs a shady corner to establish well.

TYPE Rhizome

FLOWERS White, late spring/early summer

FRUITS Small red berries, late summer

HEIGHT 15–20cm (6–8in)

SPREAD 60cm (24in)

PLANTING Plant crowns 8cm (3in) apart, singly or in groups, in early autumn

SITE Full or partial shade, under deciduous trees, in shrub borders or woodland

SOIL Prefers a soil containing leaf mould which will retain moisture and prevent the roots from drying out

CARE Mulch around the plants in spring with leaf mould or garden compost. Lift and divide overgrown clumps in autumn or late winter, if necessary

PROPAGATION Lily of the valley spreads naturally by its underground rhizomes. New plants can be made by dividing and replanting the crowns in autumn or late winter

WILDLIFE An increasingly uncommon plant in the wild, it is a useful component of a woodland habitat

WILD CHERRY (*Prunus avium*)

Sometimes known by its older name of 'gean', the wild cherry forms a spreading tree which is only really suited to the largest gardens. It is the parent of most of the fruiting and ornamental cherries in cultivation and is grown not only for its flowers and fruit but also for the crimson colour of the leaves in autumn.

TYPE Deciduous tree

FLOWERS White, mid- to late spring

FRUITS Yellow, red or black berries, sweet or bitter, late summer

HEIGHT 18m (60ft)

SPREAD 6–8m (20–25ft)

PLANTING Plant young trees, 1–2m (3–6½ft) high, between late autumn and early spring, when the ground is workable

SITE In woodland or as an individual specimen tree. Plant at least 27m (90ft) away from the nearest building

SOIL Fertile, well-drained soil preferred, but will tolerate most ordinary garden soils

CARE No regular pruning required

PROPAGATION In the wild, the cherry spreads by throwing up suckers from its base, which are clones of the parent plant. Occasionally the stones are planted by birds and may germinate some way away from the parent tree. In the garden, propagation is by seed. Sow cherry stones outdoors in pots as soon as the fruit has ripened and allow the cold weather to encourage germination

VARIETIES *P. avium* 'Plena' is one of the most popular cultivars, growing to a height of 12m (40ft). It has masses of double white flowers, but the fruits are rarely set

WILDLIFE Wild cherry depends on bees and hoverflies working the flowers for its pollination. The flowers also attract several species of butterfly, particularly peacocks. It supports a range of native beetles and the fruit is popular with birds

DWARF CHERRY

If space is limited there is a native dwarf cherry (Prunus cerasus) which will serve the wildlife equally well. As a shrub it grows no higher than 5m (15ft) and can be incorporated in hedges or a shrub border. It bears pinkish-white flowers and has acid-tasting red berries.

GARDEN ALLIUMS

Summer-flowering alliums are easy to grow and worth a special place in the wildlife garden. Unlike ramsons garlic (*A. ursinum*), they need a sunny spot and a well-drained soil. *Allium sphaerocephalon* has rounded heads of dark red flowers, irresistible to tortoiseshell butterflies. The striking *Allium giganteum*, growing to 1.2m (4ft) or more, has purple flowerheads that act as a magnet to bees, butterflies and flying insects. Plant the bulbs in early autumn for flowers in early summer.

BIRD CHERRY (*Prunus padus*)

A smaller relative of the wild cherry, this tree may have got its common name because of the fruit which, although bitter to human taste, is eaten by birds. A common native of woods and hedgerows.

TYPE Deciduous tree or shrub

FLOWERS White, late spring

FRUITS Black cherries, bitter, late summer

HEIGHT 15m (50ft)

SPREAD 5–6m (15–20ft)

PLANTING Plant young trees, 1–2m (3–6½ft) high, between autumn and early spring, when the weather allows

SITE In woodland or shrub borders

SOIL Any well drained

CARE No pruning required

PROPAGATION By seed taken from the ripened fruit (see Wild Cherry)

VARIETIES The most common cultivated variety, 'Watereri', has longer, drooping flowerheads

WILDLIFE Heavily scented racemes of blossom invite a number of flying insects. Fruit is quickly picked off by the birds, particularly blackbirds

PLANTING A NATIVE HEDGE

Hedges have been an integral part of the cultivated landscape in Britain since at least Anglo-Saxon times and may even date back as far as the Bronze Age. Different types of hedges were planted for different purposes: a double hedge, for example, would mark an important boundary whilst a hedge designed to contain livestock would be particularly impenetrable at the base. Almost incidentally they became shelters and pathways for wildlife, harbouring birds, mammals and insects. In the garden, a hedge of native species can serve both as a wildlife provider and as an effective division between neighbouring plots.

HEDGING PLANTS

CANES AND STRING

TRENCH

PLANTING TIMES

Container-grown hedging plants can be planted at any time during the year, except when the ground is baked hard or frozen. However, the best time for planting evergreens is late spring and the best time for deciduous species is late autumn. Bare-root plants should only be put in when they are dormant, between late autumn and early spring.

CHOOSING THE SPECIES

Monoculture – the planting of only one species in a hedge – is accepted gardening practice. Native species like yew, beech, holly and hawthorn have traditionally been used to make garden boundaries and although they make indisputably fine hedges, their use as a wildlife corridor is limited. A mixed hedge, on the other hand, provides a much wider resource and a greater number of animal and flower species will soon become associated with it. A balanced hedge might include a large proportion of one of the mainstay species such as hawthorn, which forms a dense, thorny structure, as well as blossoms and berries. This may be interspersed with four or five other species which flower and fruit at different times, and should include at least one evergreen to provide shelter in winter.

TREES/SHRUBS SUITABLE FOR HEDGING

PLANT	DESCRIPTION
ALDER BUCKTHORN (*Frangula alnus*)	Deciduous, fruit
BEECH (*Fagus sylvatica*)	Slow-growing, deciduous, autumn colour
BLACKTHORN (*Prunus spinosa*)	Deciduous, blossom, fruit
CRAB APPLE (*Malus sylvestris*)	Deciduous, blossom, fruit
DOG ROSE (*Rosa canina*)	Deciduous, blossom, hips
ELM (*Ulmus procera*)	Deciduous
FIELD MAPLE (*Acer campestre*)	Deciduous, autumn colour
HAWTHORN (*Crataegus monogyna*)	Deciduous, blossom, berries
HAZEL (*Corylus avellana*)	Deciduous, catkins, nuts
HOLLY (*Ilex aquifolium*)	Slow-growing, evergreen, berries
WILD PRIVET (*Ligustrum ovalifolium*)	Quick-growing, evergreen
YEW (*Taxus baccata*)	Slow-growing, evergreen

HOW TO PLANT A HEDGE

1. Choose two-year-old seedlings, which are large enough to handle, but should not need staking.

2. Mark out the length of the hedge with canes and string. It does not have to be a straight line, a curving hedge works just as well.

3. Dig a trench in front of the line, 60cm (2ft) wide and 45cm (18in) deep, running the entire length of the proposed hedge. Remove weed roots and large stones whilst digging.

4. Add a layer of organic matter (garden compost or well-rotted manure) and mix with the loose soil at the bottom of the trench.

5. Set the plants, 30–45cm (12–18in) apart and at the same depth as they were in the nursery (shown by the soil mark on the stem), adding more soil to the bottom of the trench, if necessary, to ensure the plant will sit at the right depth.

6. Holding the plant upright, fill around the roots with loose soil, until it reaches the soil mark on the stem, firming down well.

IMMEDIATE AFTERCARE

Water the new plants thoroughly, making sure the water soaks down around the roots. Cut back the top and side growths by at least one third – this will encourage side branching and bushy growth.

ANCIENT HEDGEROWS

We often hear and read of 'ancient hedgerows', but just how old are the hedges we see in the countryside today? The Anglo-Saxons certainly planted mixed hedgerows which incorporated naturally growing trees and shrubs as well as specially planted ones. However, most of the hedges we see today were laid out between 1750 and 1850 – the so-called 'Enclosure' years, when large open areas were enclosed to make the smaller, rectangular fields we know today – involving the planting of some 320,000 kilometres (200,000 miles) of hedging. The earlier hedges contained a wide range of species, but for economic reasons enclosure hedges were normally one species only – usually hawthorn (*Crataegus monogyna*).

MAINTENANCE

Each spring, whilst the hedge is still forming, prune the top and side shoots by one third. Do not leave the central stem to grow to the desired height of the hedge before cutting back. Regular pruning will ensure that by the time the hedge does reach its final height, it will have developed a strong, dense framework.

It is a good idea to apply a mulch of garden compost, leaf mould or chopped bark around the plants each spring. This will discourage weeds (which may strangle the young hedge) and form a good environment for hedgerow plants and microscopic creatures.

CLIPPING

The main difference between conventional hedge care and those managed for wildlife is in the clipping. Wildlife hedges should never be clipped before nesting is completely finished; usually it is safe to do so in late summer or early autumn, but if in doubt, leave until the winter when the deciduous species are dormant. (For details on evergreen hedges, see tasks for the month of August.)

WILDLIFE TO EXPECT

Blackbirds, thrushes, dunnocks, sparrows, greenfinches and bullfinches all prefer the dense, protected growth of a hedge to any other nesting site. They will be joined in the summer by shy, ground-feeding wrens, who search the leaf litter beneath the hedge for spiders and other insects. Many other garden birds like tits and robins will use the hedge simply as a convenient perch, for picking off caterpillars from the leafy growth. The hedge foliage is a particularly good breeding ground for moths such as the privet hawkmoth, garden spiders who leave their mark in the shape of finely woven webs, and the often heard, but rarely seen, bush cricket. At ground level, the wildlife residents are most likely to be hedgehogs, woodmice and bank voles, although toads and frogs often hide in the shelter of a hedge bottom. In time a native hedge will become a busy wildlife corridor offering shelter, food and a convenient route from one part of the garden to another.

HEDGEROW FLOWERS

Although the soil at the base of the hedge may be poor, a surprising number of wildflowers seem to thrive there. The orientation of the hedge will determine which flowers may be grown. South-facing hedges receive a good deal of sun whilst north faces may be in almost complete shade. Choose a selection of plants to suit the position of your hedge.

Most of the hedgerow flowers tolerate a dry, poor soil, but one or two such as primroses and lesser celandines need to be kept moist. Unless the hedge is by a stream or pool, it is unlikely that their needs will be met; they would be happier in a damp ditch or marshy area.

Pot-grown plants can be planted out any time from spring to autumn. In the first two years of the hedge's growth, avoid putting in the taller plants, such as sweet cicely (*Myrrhis odorata*), which may compete with the new hedging. It is also advisable to wait until the hedge is well-established (five years or more) before putting in hedgerow climbers, like traveller's joy (*Clematis vitalba*). Its scrambling habit is ideal for dense, well-grown hedges, but it can easily strangle younger plants. It is best to use small, healthy plants for the hedge bottom and not seedlings, whose roots may not be sufficiently developed to cope with the poor soil. Insert the new plants with a trowel and water thoroughly. Water regularly for the first two weeks particularly if there is a hot, dry spell.

WILDLIFE USES FOR HEDGING

Caterpillars of brimstone butterflies feed on alder buckthorn

Blackthorn, hawthorn, hazel and privet provide nectar for many species of butterfly

Thrushes, dunnocks, garden warblers and finches use the hedgerow for nesting

Hedgehogs, voles and woodmice shelter and feed in the hedge bottom

Hawthorn, blackthorn and holly provide berries for birds in winter

RECOMMENDED NATIVE HEDGEROW FLOWERS

PLANT	TYPE	POSITION	SOIL	WILDLIFE VALUE
BETONY (*Stachys officinalis*)	Perennial	Sun or shade	Any	Bees, butterflies
BLUEBELL (*Scilla non-scripta*)	Bulb	Sun or shade	Any	Bees, butterflies
COMMON DOG VIOLET (*Viola riviana*)	Perennial	Partial shade	Any	Caterpillar food plant for fritillary butterflies
GARLIC MUSTARD (*Alliaria petiolata*)	Biennial	Partial shade	Any	Caterpillar food plant for orange tips, tortoiseshells and whites
GREATER STITCHWORT (*Stellaria holostea*)	Perennial	Partial shade	Any	Bees, moths, butterflies
HEDGE WOUNDWORT (*Stachys sylvatica*)	Perennial	Partial shade	Any	Bees, butterflies
HEDGEROW CRANESBILL (*Geranium pyrenaicum*)	Perennial	Partial shade	Any	
LESSER CELANDINE (*Ranunculus ficaria*)	Perennial	Partial shade	Damp	Bees, butterflies
PRIMROSE (*Primula vulgaris*)	Perennial	Sun or shade	Damp	Butterflies (whites)
RED CAMPION (*Silene dioica*)	Perennial	Sun or shade	Any	Butterflies
SELFHEAL (*Prunella vulgaris*)	Perennial	Sun or shade	Any	Bees, butterflies
SWEET CICELY (*Myrrhis odorata*)	Perennial	Sun or shade	Any	Bees
WHITE DEADNETTLE (*Lamium album*)	Perennial	Sun or shade	Any	Bees

JUNE

By early summer most of the garden's wildlife are busy bringing up their young. In the pond, tadpoles are turning into adults and are at their most vulnerable as they emerge from the water and seek shelter from predators amongst the marginal plants. Resident garden birds like blackbirds are starting their second brood, although newly arrived migrants like the garden warblers have yet to mate. Bats produce their single offspring this month and the adults can be seen swooping around the house and garden at dusk to feed.

Young hedgehogs are also being born now in litters of four or five. Although born blind, within two weeks their eyes will be open and the brown adult spines starting to develop. The parents feed at night and can often be heard shuffling around the garden in the darkness. This is the best time to watch for fox cubs, as they leave the safety of the earth to explore their immediate surroundings.

A healthy garden pond will be home to large numbers of dragonflies and damselflies. There are around forty different species in Britain and their spectacular wings and dazzling colours make good viewing. Often, the only way to tell the difference between the two insects is to watch them in flight – the gentle flutter of the damselfly in contrast to the dragonfly's powerful darting movements. The aerial acrobatic displays denote mating, and before long eggs will be laid just under the water, frequently on the stems of aquatic plants.

For traditional gardeners, summer means roses. In the wildlife garden, too, many of the native shrub roses come in to flower. They demand far less attention than their hybrid counterparts and are equally effective in providing nectar and hips for insects and birds.

TASKS FOR THE MONTH

- [ ] Feed hedgehogs
- [ ] Lift and divide spring-flowering bulbs
- [ ] Clear pond of algae and pondweed
- [ ] Cut down the nettle patch
- [ ] Sow biennial seeds outdoors
- [ ] Cut spring-flowering meadow
- [ ] Divide irises

FEEDING HEDGEHOGS

In dry spells, when slugs, snails and worms may not be so easy to come by, garden hedgehogs can be given an artificial diet boost. This is particularly important now, when the babies are being born and the females are suckling and unable to travel far for food. Put out a saucer of tinned pet food and one of water each night in a regular spot. Don't feed bread and milk which upsets the hedgehog's digestive system.

LIFTING AND DIVIDING BULBS

When spring bulbs have finished flowering and the leaves have begun to die back, they can be divided. Choose clumps that have been undisturbed for at least three years: a poor show of flowers indicates that the bulbs are becoming congested. This method is applicable to grape hyacinths, bluebells, snakeshead fritillary, ramsons garlic, daffodils, crocuses and tulips.

- Insert a fork well clear of the clump and push it down deeply to come up under the bulbs. Gently ease the complete clump out of the ground. Remove the excess soil and discard any bulbs which are soft or rotten. Detach the small bulbs and the bulbils for replanting.

- Replant the large bulbs immediately at normal planting depth (see tasks for the month of October for guidance). The small bulbs should also be planted straight away at two thirds of their usual planting depth. The tiny bulbils only need to be covered with their own depth of soil. Small bulbs will not flower in their first year and bulbils may take up to four years to reach maturity, so it is a good idea to put them into a separate nursery bed.

- Alternatively, they can be planted directly amongst the existing bulbs, where they will eventually create a denser display, but remember to allow enough room for each bulb to develop to its full size.

CLEARING THE POND

Warm weather leads to a growth of pondweed and algae, which can choke the pond if not checked. Don't be tempted to use chemicals which will indiscriminately kill the water creatures. Rake the excess growth out with a garden rake, and lay it by the side of the pond for a day or so. This allows at least some of the insects and water snails to find their way back to the water. Then add the vegetation to the compost heap.

CUTTING DOWN THE NETTLE PATCH

If a small part of the garden has been developed as a stinging nettle patch (see July), cut down half of the plants now to provide new growth for the next generation of butterflies. Small tortoiseshells, peacocks, commas and red admirals will lay their eggs on the shoots to make sure that the emerging caterpillars are well supplied with a diet of young nettle leaves.

SOWING SEEDS OF BIENNIALS

Many useful flowering plants can be started off now from seed. Biennials sown now and planted out in the autumn will flower next spring or summer, for one year only.

Sowing biennials

Biennial seeds may be sown either in pots or, if there is room, in nursery beds in the garden. Pots should be filled with seed compost and the soil in the bed raked to a fine texture. Both soil and compost should be moist before sowing. Choose a lightly shaded position to protect the new seedlings from the heat of the summer sun.

Sow the seeds, thinly spaced and about 1cm (½in) deep. In beds this can be done by sprinkling the seed and then raking lightly to ensure that the seed lies just beneath the surface of the soil. In pots, seeds can be pressed lightly into the compost by hand. Water well, using a watering-can fitted with a fine sprinkler rose. Remember to mark the positions of the different species.

Aftercare

Six weeks after sowing, crowded seedlings should be thinned out and transplanted to additional pots or beds. Young plants must never be allowed to dry out. In mid-summer, pinch out the tip of each plant to encourage bushy growth. Plant out the grown plants in mid-autumn to their permanent flowering positions.

BIENNIALS

Evening primrose (*Oenothera biennis*) B, M, H
Flowers – early summer to mid-autumn

Forget-me-not (*Myosotis sylvatica*) N, B, Nat
Flowers – mid-spring to mid-summer

Foxglove (*Digitalis purpurea*) B, Po, Nat
Flowers – early to mid-summer

Great mullein (*Verbascum thapsus*) B, Nat
Flowers – summer

Honesty (*Lunaria biennis*) N, S
Flowers – mid-spring to early summer

Sweet rocket (*Hesperis matronalis*) N, Nat
Flowers – early summer

Sweet William (*Dianthus barbatus*) N
Flowers – early summer

Teasel (*Dipsacus fullonum*) N, B, S, Nat
Flowers – late summer

Wallflower (*Cheiranthus cheiri*) N, Nat
Flowers – late spring

FLEDGLING BIRDS

Don't be tempted to 'rescue' baby birds which appear to have been abandoned by their parents. It is likely that they have fallen from the nest before they are able to fly and the parents are near at hand, feeding them at regular intervals. If they are in danger from cars, move them out of the way under the nearest shrub or tree and then leave them well alone. The parent birds will be waiting nearby to return to their offspring.

CUTTING THE SPRING-FLOWERING MEADOW

Established wildflower lawns or meadows which have been managed specifically for spring-flowering plants like cowslips and fritillaries can be cut once they have finished. This is at the expense of summer-flowering species but enables the grass to be used as a conventional lawn for the rest of the season.

Use a sturdy rotary mower or strimmer and cut back to 10cm (4in) high. Leave the cuttings on the grass for a day or so, to allow insects and seeds time to find their way back to ground. Rake off and add the clippings (sparingly) to the compost heap.

WARNING

Power tools can be dangerous if not handled properly. If in doubt, get professional help.

DIVIDING IRISES

Bearded garden irises (*Iris germanica*) and the native yellow flag iris (*Iris pseudacorus*) can be lifted and divided now if they have become overcrowded.

· After flowering, lift the clumps out of the soil with a fork.

· Select healthy young pieces of rhizome and cut them away from the main clump with a knife. Discard the older parts from the centre.

· Cut back the leaves to 23cm (9in) to make them more stable in the wind.

· Replant the new pieces so that the rhizome just shows above the soil.

· Ensure newly-planted rhizomes have an adequate supply of water until their roots have re-established themselves.

ROSES FOR A WILDLIFE GARDEN

Roses tend to be used as specimen plants, grown in isolated beds for their prize blooms, and seem to be of little relevance to the wildlife gardener. Yet several of the species and wild roses are really useful in the wildlife garden, as part of the underlayer in the woodland, as hedges or as part of a conventional shrub border. Shrub roses are versatile and the blooms are just as pleasing (if somewhat smaller) than the hybrid teas and floribundas. The simple flowers provide easily accessible pollen for bumble bees and hoverflies, plus colourful hips for birds, foxes and woodmice in the autumn. Even the leaves have a use for one type of bee, the female leaf-cutter, who cuts out semi-circular pieces of leaf to line her nest.

FOLIAGE

RHIZOME

ROOTS

Plants of the Month

HONEYSUCKLE (*Lonicera periclymenum*)

Also known as woodbine, the native honeysuckle is frequently seen in hedgerows or growing amongst shrubs in woodland.

TYPE Deciduous climber

HABIT Scrambling, twining stems

FLOWERS White, tinged with purple, summer

FRUITS Red berries, autumn

HEIGHT To 6m (20ft)

PLANTING Plant in autumn or early spring

SITE Sun or light shade. Against a wall, fence or trellis, over an arch or pergola, through a hedge or old tree

SOIL Any, well-drained soil

CARE No special care needed. Mulch of well-rotted manure or compost can be put around roots in spring, but is not essential. Regular pruning not required. Remove old wood from overgrown specimens after flowering

PROPAGATION Hardwood cuttings taken in early to mid-autumn. Seed can be collected from ripe berries

WILDLIFE The strong night-time scent is attractive to hawkmoths. During the day, only long-tongued bumble bees can reach the nectar in the trumpet-shaped flowers. In spring, the new shoots are popular with blackfly, which in turn provide food for ladybirds, lacewings and baby birds. Strips of bark are taken by birds for nest building. In autumn the berries are eaten by birds (note they are poisonous to humans)

RAGGED ROBIN (*Lychnis flos-cuculi*)

This pretty native plant of wet meadows and marshland is a good garden plant for damp soils and wetlands. 'Ragged' probably refers to the petals which are cut into segments, giving a fringed, ragged appearance.

TYPE Perennial

FLOWERS Pink, early summer

HEIGHT 60cm (2ft)

PLANTING Put out young plants in spring or autumn

SITE Sun or partial shade, wetlands, pond margins, damp meadows

SOIL Moist, fertile

CARE Cut back flowering stems in mid-summer (after flowering) to encourage a second flush of flowers in late summer

PROPAGATION Self-seeds readily. Plants may also be increased by division in spring

WILDLIFE Long-tongued bees, flies and many species of butterflies (including whites and the common blue) seek out the pollen and nectar. Ragged robin is an essential ingredient of wetlands and marshy pool margins

WILD AND SPECIES SHRUB ROSES

TYPE	ABOUT	FLOWERS/ FLOWER SIZE	HIPS	HEIGHT/ SPREAD	USES
Rosa rugosa	Introduced from China, but widely naturalised in Britain and Europe. Heavily scented blooms	Deep pink, mid- to late summer 4–8cm (1½–3in), solitary	Large, orange- red, early autumn	1.8m (6ft) height 1.2m (4ft) spread	Hedging, shrub borders
Dog rose (Rosa canina)	The most common native rose, found growing wild in hedgerows and on roadsides	Pale pink or white, mid- summer 5cm (2in), in clusters	Red, autumn	2.5m (8ft) height 1.8m (6ft) spread	Hedging, woodland edge
Rosa glauca (syn. R. rubrifolia)	Native to central and southern Europe, but widely grown in British gardens for its purple- grey foliage, dark stems and abundant hips. Look out for self-sown seedlings	Purplish-pink, mid-summer 4cm (1½in), in clusters	Reddish- brown when ripe, autumn	2.2m (7ft) height 1.5m (5ft) spread	Woodland edge, shrub border
Sweet briar (Rosa rubiginosa)	Another native wild rose of scrub and grass banks. Leaves have a strong apple scent when crushed	Bright pink, in small clusters, mid-summer 2.5cm (1in)	Bright red, autumn	2.5m (8ft) height 2.5m (8ft) spread	Hedging, shrub borders, woodland edge

CULTIVATION OF WILD AND SPECIES SHRUB ROSES

PLANTING Plant new bushes between late autumn and early spring, when the ground is not too hard. Add garden compost or well-rotted manure to the planting hole. Set hedging plants 30–45cm (12–18in) apart

SITE Sun or light shade

SOIL Any, well-drained soil

CARE No regular pruning needed, but untidy bushes or hedges can be trimmed in late winter. Take out weak stems at ground level and remove straggly growing tips. Mulch in spring with garden compost or leaf mould

PROPAGATION From cuttings taken in late summer/early autumn

FIELD ROSE (ROSA ARVENSIS)

Found growing in the hedgerows and woodlands at the margins of fields rather than in the fields themselves. It is a widespread native rose in Britain, bearing solitary white flowers throughout the summer.

COMMON EVENING PRIMROSE
(*Oenothera biennis*)

Originating from North America, the evening primrose has become naturalised on waste ground, embankments and verges. It is not related to the primrose family (*Primula*) and was probably named because of the similarity in colour. All species produce a mass of flowers but each flower only lasts a day, opening in the evening to give off a light fragrance.

TYPE Biennial

FLOWERS Yellow, summer/early autumn

HEIGHT 1m (3ft)

PLANTING Plant out in autumn or spring, 30cm (12in) apart

SITE Full sun, in borders

SOIL Well drained

CARE No special care needed

PROPAGATION Self-seeds easily. Seed may be sown in late spring or early summer to flower the following year (seeds sometimes germinate and flower the same year)

RELATED The large-flowered evening primrose (*O. glaxioviana*) is a taller plant of about 1.5m (5ft), and it is easily identifiable by its large flowers and red hairs on the stem

WILDLIFE Evening primroses rely on moths for their pollination, hence the nocturnal opening hours of the flowers. The moths are attracted by the pale colour and also by the scent and are rewarded with nectar. Although the flowers only open at dusk, they usually last until noon the next day, allowing hoverflies time to visit the plant

FOXGLOVE (*Digitalis purpurea*)

A tall-growing native of open woodlands and scrub. *D. purpurea* is very poisonous and the drug extracted from the plant is still used to treat heart conditions.

TYPE Biennial

FLOWERS Pink to purple, and occasionally white, spotted interior, early to mid-summer

HEIGHT 1.2m (4ft)

PLANTING Plant foxgloves between mid-autumn and early spring

SITE Partial shade, in open woodlands, or shady borders

SOIL Any, moist

CARE No special care needed

PROPAGATION From seed sown in early to mid-summer

WILDLIFE The leaves provide food for butterfly caterpillars; the flowers are visited by pollen-seeking bumble bees

PLANTING WALLS AND ROCK BANKS

In natural conditions, a dry, rocky landscape hosts a diverse collection of plants and animals which are specific to this terrain. Very few gardens incorporate a cliff or mountain slope but it is possible to recreate these habitats on a smaller scale, particularly if the garden already includes an old wall, or rockery. Even paths and paving stones can be interplanted with species that prefer a shallow soil and new walls can be adapted to 'take' new species.

There are several good reasons for incorporating this kind of specialised habitat into a wildlife garden. Many of the native rock plants are becoming rare in the countryside and the garden can play an important conservation role. The habitat will also greatly increase the range of wildlife that use the garden, some of which will only be attracted to the dry conditions and specialised plants that grow here. Rock plants are amongst some of the prettiest species and for that reason alone they deserve to be grown.

WALL WILDLIFE CENTRES

Old brick or stone walls are excellent wildlife 'centres'. Plants root and flourish in the soft lime mortar just as they would in the crevices of limestone rocks in the wild. New walls, held together with cement rather than mortar, tend to have less plant growth, but with time and weathering the cement will soften and allow seedlings to get a hold and grow on.

Even without planting, older walls may host a range of mosses, various types of lichen and, where the air is moist, ferns like wall rue and the maidenhair spleenwort. Larger plants like elder and buddleia are often found clinging precariously high on town walls, their seeds having been deposited there by birds.

A good wall creates its own microclimate, usually warmer than the surrounding garden, where wall butterflies and hawkmoths will bask in the reflected warmth. Spiders and beetles use the crevices to keep cool and solitary mason bees and wasps make chambers in the mortar. A wall top is often used by birds as a boundary to their territory; blackbirds and robins are

particularly territorial and will sit on top of the wall to warn off their rivals with noisy displays of aggression. Old walls with loose bricks may house hole-nesting wrens, robins, great tits, redstarts or spotted flycatchers.

PLANTING IN A WALL

The best walls are low and loosely constructed with plenty of gaps and pockets for planting. Most plants prefer some soil, however poor or shallow, and this can be added where necessary. It is best to put in young plants in spring or autumn and water well until established. If the crevices between the stones are very small, individual seeds or seedlings can be planted instead. In time, the plants will self-seed and spread. See Flowering Wall Plants table for a list of suitable plants.

FLOWERING WALL PLANTS

PLANT	SEASON	HEIGHT	FLOWERS
SMALL-LEAVED COTONEASTER (*C. microphyllus*) F	Summer	6cm (2½in) (2m/6ft spread)	White (scarlet berries)
HOARY CINQUEFOIL (*Potentilla argentea*) N, B	Summer to early autumn	30cm (12in)	Yellow
HOUSELEEK (*Sempervivum tectorum*) I	Summer	8cm (3in)	Red-purple
IVY-LEAVED TOADFLAX (*Cymbalaria muralis*) N, B	Summer	10cm (4in) trailing	Lilac with yellow markings
LONDON PRIDE (*Saxifraga x urbinum*) N	Summer	15cm (6in)	Pink
RED VALERIAN (*Centranthus ruber*) Nat	Summer	60cm (24in)	Red, pink or white
ROUND-LEAVED CRANESBILL (*Geranium rotundifolium*) Nat	Summer	15cm (6in)	Pink
BITING STONECROP (*Sedum acre*) Nat, N	Summer	10cm (4in)	Yellow
WHITE STONECROP (*Sedum album*) Nat, N	Summer	10cm (4in)	White
WALLFLOWER (*Cheiranthus cheiri*) N, Nat	Spring to early summer	30cm (12in)	Yellow to orange-brown
WALL ROCKET (*Diplotaxis tenuifolia*) B, Nat	Late spring to early autumn	60cm (24in)	Yellow
ARABIS (*Arabis albida*) B, N	Late spring to mid-summer	15cm (6in)	White
YELLOW CORYDALIS (*Corydalis lutea*)	Summer to early autumn	15cm (6in)	Yellow

PLANTING IN GRAVEL AND PAVING

Many plants enjoy the dry growing conditions and reflected warmth of gravel, stone chippings or paving. It is relatively easy to incorporate native species into existing paving schemes or to lay areas of gravel in which to site them.

MAKING A GRAVEL BED

- The underlying soil should be well-drained and gritty. If it is too heavy, mix it with equal parts of rock chippings or gravel.

- Cover the area with a layer of sand 2.5cm (1in) in depth.

- Finish the bed with a 2.5cm (1in) layer of gravel or 0.5cm (¼in) stone chippings.

- Water plants well before removing them from their pots. Use a narrow trowel to make holes the same size as the root ball of the plants and firm them in gently.

- Water new plants thoroughly and sprinkle more gravel over the surface if necessary.

SELF-SEEDING

Many plants will self-seed readily in gravel, so that in a short space of time the gravel will have a natural, 'unplanted' appearance. Any weeds that also self-seed freely, such as groundsel, can be removed by hand.

RECOMMENDED PLANTS FOR GRAVEL, TROUGHS AND ROCK GARDENS

PLANT	FLOWER	HEIGHT	WILDLIFE VALUE
CHEDDAR PINK (*Dianthus gratianopolitanus*) Nat, R	Early summer	20cm (8in)	Moths, butterflies
COMMON PINK (*Dianthus plumarius*) Nat	Summer	20cm (8in)	Bees
HAIRY THYME (*Thymus praecox*) Nat	Summer	8–10cm (3–4in)	Bees
HAREBELL (*Campanula rotundifolia*) Nat	Late summer	30cm (12in)	Bees
HEBE 'AUTUMN GLORY'	Autumn	60–90cm (2–3ft) (60–90cm/2–3ft spread)	Butterflies
HEBE 'CARL TESCHNER'	Summer	30cm (12in) (60–90cm/2–3ft spread)	Hoverflies, bees
HERB ROBERT (*Geranium robertianum*) Nat	Summer	30cm (12in)	Bees
LING (HEATHER) (*Calluna vulgaris*) Nat	Late summer	30–60cm (12–24in)	Ground cover for birds, grass snakes and slow worms
PURPLE SAXIFRAGE (*Saxifraga oppositifolia*) Nat	Summer	8cm (3in)	Butterflies, bees
ROCK ROSE (*Helianthemum nummularium*) Nat	Summer	15cm (6in) (60cm/24in spread)	Bees, insects
SPRING GENTIAN (*Gentiana verna*) Nat, R	Spring	8cm (3in)	Butterflies, bees

PLANTING IN PAVING

If new paths or patios are to be laid, it is worth considering leaving some gaps between the paving stones as planting pockets. If the stones are already laid, it is still possible to incorporate a wide range of species. The simplest way is to take up some of the stones, perhaps to create a chequerboard effect. This is better done in a random pattern, rather than taking out every other stone. The earth beneath the stones should be workable and weed-free. Dig out the earth to a depth of 15–23cm (6–9in) and mix with an equal quantity of gravel or stone chippings. Replace the soil mixture and plant in the normal way. Brick paths or patios can be planted in the same way. Take out any bricks that are already damaged or crumbling and fill the gaps as described before.

PLANTS FOR PAVING AND GRAVEL

The following plants will thrive in a shallow, well-drained soil in full sun and will self-seed easily:

Broom (*Cytisus scoparius*) Nat, B

Common toadflax (*Linaria vulgaris*) Nat, B

Globe thistle (*Echinops sphaerocephalus*) B, N

Great mullein (*Verbascum phlomoides*) Nat, I

Hawkweed (*Hieracium murorum*) Nat

Lady's bedstraw (*Galium verum*) Nat

Maiden pink (*Dianthus deltoides*) Nat

Thyme (*Thymus* spp. especially the native *Thymus praecox*) B

Trailing St John's wort (*Hypericum humifusum*) Nat

White campion (*Silene latifolia*) Nat

Yarrow (*Achillea millefolium*) Nat

JULY

Food supplies are plentiful this month at every level of the garden ecosystem. As the flower borders reach their peak, nectar keeps bees and butterflies contented and new generations of caterpillars feed on the abundant leaves. At ground level the rising population of slugs and beetles is quickly devoured by young hedgehogs. Fox cubs, now above ground after several months in the earth, are practising their hunting skills on garden voles and mice. So-called pests like aphids and midges are also at their peak but are scooped up in huge numbers by bats, blue tits and swallows.

But it is at night that the garden really comes to life. So many of the night-scented plants are in flower now, beckoning moths and butterflies with their sweet smell. Honeysuckle, evening primrose, night-scented stock and nicotiana attract not only with their scent, but also with their pale light-reflecting colours. Bat watching can also be rewarding, with possible sunset sightings of the larger noctules and, in the south of Britain, serotines.

Although there is plenty of food available, garden wildlife can suffer in hot dry spells from lack of water. Pond levels drop and marshy areas may dry out altogether. In the long term, the wetland habitat will not suffer as long as rain comes in the autumn, but extra dishes of water and bird baths are always welcome.

Native plants tend to be more resilient to dry spells than garden hybrids, although there are exceptions; imports from the Mediterranean like rosemary and thyme will positively thrive in a near-drought situation. A wildlife garden does not usually need constant attention and as long as water supplies can be maintained, gardeners may go off on holiday with an easy mind.

TASKS FOR THE MONTH

- [ ] Water hanging baskets and containers daily
- [ ] Plant autumn-flowering bulbs
- [ ] Prune broom
- [ ] Cut the summer-flowering meadow
- [ ] Tie in climbers
- [ ] Trim rock plants
- [ ] Prune rambler roses
- [ ] Feed container plants
- [ ] Undertake a butterfly count

WATERING

It is vital to keep bird baths and water bowls topped up during the summer months. Pay special attention to container-grown plants and hanging baskets, which will need watering daily to prevent plants from dehydrating.

PLANTING AUTUMN-FLOWERING BULBS

The meadow saffron (Colchicum autumnale) – sometimes called autumn crocus – and the true autumn-flowering crocus (Crocus speciosus) can be planted now. Both species look best grown in bold groups, in well-drained soil and in an open position or under a deciduous tree. Use a trowel or specially designed bulb planter and set the bulbs 10cm (4in) deep and 20cm (8in) apart for colchicums, 10cm (4in) deep and 10cm (4in) apart for crocuses. Cover completely with earth and firm in place.

SOWING BIENNIALS

It is not too late to sow seeds of biennial plants for flowering next spring and summer. Wallflowers, foxgloves, forget-me-not and sweet rocket may be sown outdoors now and put into their flowering positions in the autumn (see tasks for the month of June for details).

PRUNE BROOM

Broom (*Cytisus scoparius*) should be pruned annually after it has finished flowering. Careful pruning will prevent the shrub becoming bare-stemmed and leggy.

- Using sharp secateurs, cut back all or most of the stems which have just flowered. You should make the cut just above the point where the stem joins the old wood and where new shoots are developing.

- Take care not to cut into the old wood, as it does not respond well to pruning and may fail to produce any new growth. Mature plants tend to become hard-wooded after several years and, if pruning has no effect, it is best to discard them.

BROOM LIFESPAN
Brooms are short-lived shrubs and should be discarded after six or seven years, when they become too woody and cease to flower.

CUTTING THE SUMMER-FLOWERING MEADOW

Established meadows

This is the traditional hay-making time of year and a good time to give the established summer-flowering lawn or meadow its annual cut. When the best of the summer flowers are over, cut down the grass to 10cm (4in), using a strimmer or scythe (both should be handled by an experienced user for safety purposes). Leave the cuttings to dry in place for a day or so, as this allows insects time to crawl back into the meadow and any seeds to fall back to ground. Then, rake off the cuttings and add (sparingly) to the compost heap.

New meadows

Meadows sown last autumn with a mixture of meadow and annual cornfield flower seeds, should also be given their annual cut this month. If the cornfield annuals are still in flower, the cut can be left for a few weeks until they have finished. New lawns and meadows sown without cornfield annuals should only be cut if particularly long and untidy (see tasks for the month of April for more details).

TYING IN CLIMBERS

New growths of climbing plants such as honeysuckle or clematis should be trained towards their wires or trellis. If they are not tied in, the shoots become tangled and may not grow in the desired direction.

TRIMMING ROCK PLANTS

In small rock gardens and walls, rock plants can soon outgrow their allotted space. As soon as they have finished flowering, cut back alyssum, aubretia, rock roses and pinks using secateurs for individual plants or shears for larger clumps, to encourage new shoots to grow from the base.

PRUNING RAMBLER ROSES

The flexible stems of rambler roses make them excellent plants for growing over banks, through trees or in hedges, where they can be allowed to scramble unaided by trellis or ties. Unlike shrub and climbing roses, they bear their best flowers on the previous year's growth. Immediately after flowering (usually this month, although some varieties may not finish until late summer), cut out the stems that have just borne flowers, leaving room for the young stems to come through. Use sharp secateurs and make clean cuts at ground level. Wear heavy duty gardening gloves to disentangle the prunings from the rest of the plant.

FEEDING CONTAINER PLANTS

This is the height of the growing season and plants in hanging baskets, tubs and window boxes should be given a liquid feed at fortnightly intervals. Alternatively, use pellets or tablets of slow-release fertiliser, which will provide enough nutrients to see the plants through to autumn.

THE BUTTERFLY COUNT

Use the garden's buddleias to carry out your own butterfly species count. It is remarkable how many will visit the flower spikes on a warm summer's day. Peacocks, tortoiseshells and red admirals are likely candidates, but painted ladies, wall browns and other less common species may well appear.

NATIVE BUTTERFLIES AND THEIR MAJOR SOURCES OF NECTAR

Brimstone Greater knapweed, thistles

Comma Michaelmas daisies, buddleia, sedum

Common blue Field scabious, greater knapweed, red campion, ragged robin

Holly blue Cotoneaster, ivy, holly

Peacock Buddleia, Michaelmas daisies, sedum

Red admiral Buddleia, Michaelmas daisies, sedum

Small tortoiseshell Buddleia, Michaelmas daisies, sedum

Speckled wood Bramble

TAKE NOTES

As the butterfly season gets into full swing, note down which plants are visited by which butterflies. Make a note to include more of these species next year.

Plants of the Month

GREATER KNAPWEED
(*Centaurea scabiosa*)

A common wildflower, found on roadsides, hedgebanks and rough grass. The knapweed makes a good garden plant, with its bold thistle-like flowers which attract a good range of insects.

TYPE Perennial

FLOWERS Mauve/purple, mid- to late summer

HEIGHT 60–90cm (2–3ft)

PLANTING Plant in early autumn or late winter

SITE In full sun, as part of a flowering meadow or in a border

SOIL Any, but prefers dry, chalky

CARE No special care needed. Border plants can be lifted and divided every four years

PROPAGATION Sow seeds as part of a meadow in early autumn. Established plants can be divided in late winter

RELATED The common knapweed (*C. nigra*) is equally useful for wildlife although it is smaller and less impressive than *C. scabiosa*. Several of the non-native garden species are hardy and make useful tall border plants, such as *C. macrocephala* which has yellow flowers

WILDLIFE The flowers are visited by bees, flying insects and particularly butterflies like brimstones. In early autumn the seedheads are eaten by finches

ROSE OF SHARON
(*Hypericum calycinum*)

Originating from Eastern Europe, *H. calycinum* is widely cultivated in gardens and naturalised in places in the countryside. As a garden plant it goes by the name of rose of Sharon but belongs to the same family as the wild St John's wort.

TYPE Evergreen sub-shrub

HABIT Carpeting

FLOWERS Yellow, summer

HEIGHT 30–45cm (12–18in)

SPREAD Indefinite

PLANTING Plant in early spring

SITE Tolerates shade but flowers better with some sun. Borders or woodland edge

SOIL Tolerates dry, poor soil. Can be grown in any well-drained garden soil

CARE Every few years, cut plants back to within several centimetres (a few inches) of the base to keep them compact

PROPAGATION *H. calycinum* spreads by horizontal creeping stems and can soon outgrow its allotted space. To make new plants, lift and divide the roots in late winter

RELATED The rock garden hypericum (*H. coris*) also appears this month and is useful for its yellow, heather-like flowers

WILDLIFE *H. calycinum* is pollinated by bees, attracted to the vivid yellow of the petals and the red-tipped anthers. It is a useful plant for a dry shady spot where it will smother weeds

COMMON (OR FIELD) POPPY
(*Papaver rhoeas*)

Formerly a frequent
sight in cultivated fields,
the common poppy
is now increasingly
confined to roadside
verges and wasteland.
It prefers ground which
has been disturbed
and occasionally makes
an unexpected en masse appearance on
motorway construction sites. In the garden
it can be used to add temporary colour to
a first year meadow or be sown with other
annual 'cornfield weeds' on a piece of
infertile ground.

TYPE Annual

FLOWERS Scarlet, summer

HEIGHT 30–45cm (12–18in)

PLANTING Plant pot-grown specimens
30cm (12in) apart in mid- to late spring
(but poppies are usually grown from seed)

SITE Full sun. Disturbed ground such as a
bonfire site or where an old shed used to
be is ideal

SOIL Prefers infertile, well-drained soil

CARE No special care needed

PROPAGATION Collect seed in late summer
or early autumn and sow immediately as
part of the flowering meadow. Alternatively
store seed for sowing outdoors in mid-
spring. Poppies self-seed very readily

WILDLIFE Attractive to hoverflies and
bees. Garden conservation is important
as the increased use of weedkillers on
agricultural land has led to their decline

NASTURTIUM (*Tropaeolum majus*)

An import from South
America, this is a
quick-growing and useful
garden plant. Trained to
climb up a trellis or allowed
to tumble over the sides of
a window box, nasturtiums
provide instant summer
colour and considerable
wildlife interest.

TYPE Annual

HABIT Climbing or trailing

FLOWERS Orange/yellow, summer

HEIGHT 2.5m (8ft)

PLANTING Set plants 40cm (16in) apart

SITE Full sun, in containers, against fences and
walls or in flower borders

SOIL Prefers poor soil. A richer soil is tolerable
but leaves may flourish at the flowers' expense

CARE Train plants up a 'wigwam' of canes or tie
into a trellis. They can also be left to trail from a
hanging basket or window box

PROPAGATION Sow seeds 2cm (¾in) deep in
their flowering position in mid-spring. Thin out
seedlings to 40cm (16in) apart

VARIETIES 'Tom Thumb' is a dwarf variety
(30cm/12in) suitable for edging paths or
growing in a rock garden

WILDLIFE Flowers attract bees and hoverflies.
Leaves are eaten by the caterpillars of the
cabbage white butterfly and other whites

MAKING A 'NO GO' AREA

However much we like to watch the comings and goings of the local wildlife, many creatures will only utilise the garden if there is one corner where they can remain totally undisturbed. It is important to nominate a part of the garden as a 'no-go' area for humans, which can be left deliberately untidy. Usually this is in some spot well away from the house and preferably shielded by shrubs or trees, but it might equally be behind a garden shed or garage.

THE WOODPILE

Old timber or unwanted logs can be piled up to provide shelter for a range of creatures. Choose a shady spot to prevent the wood from drying out in the sun. If possible, use a mixture of native woods such as elm, oak or ash which will guarantee a wider range of insect species. Logs 15–23cm (6–9in) in diameter make a good pile. The first wildlife to inhabit the pile will probably be fungi in the early autumn, but in time it will become home to spiders, beetles, wood wasps, solitary bees, slugs and snails. These will then attract bird predators, particularly wrens and blackbirds. The insects will also provide food for woodmice, voles and hedgehogs. First-year newts, after leaving the pond, may well spend time in the damp shelter of a log pile.

HEDGEHOG HABITATS

If hedgehogs are to take up residence in the garden, they need a dry, secure place for hibernation from late autumn to early spring. A pile of dead leaves or garden prunings heaped into a corner will often be acceptable, but it is also possible to construct a hibernation 'box'.

1. Use an upturned wooden box (untreated wood) and cut an entrance out of one of the side panels, 10–12cm (4–5in) square. This is large enough to allow the hedgehog to enter but small enough to prevent dogs or foxes getting in.

2. A covered entrance tunnel can also be constructed using two rows of house bricks stood on their sides and a plank of wood. Other designs with more permanent tunnels are provided by the British Hedgehog Preservation Society (see Resources).

3. Cover the box with a sheet of polythene to keep out the rain, and a mound of dry leaves or brushwood to disguise the exterior. Add a handful of straw or dry leaves as bedding.

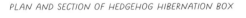

PLAN AND SECTION OF HEDGEHOG HIBERNATION BOX

HEDGEHOGS
It is very worthwhile encouraging hedgehogs to your garden as they will feed on slugs and help to keep pests under control.

NETTLE PATCH

Stinging nettles are the caterpillar food plants for several native butterflies including commas, peacocks, red admirals and small tortoiseshell. Nettles can be introduced if they are not growing naturally. In late winter, dig up some roots about 4in (10cm) long which are bearing young shoots. Bury the roots in pots of garden soil and keep cutting back the shoots to 3in (7.5cm). By late spring the new plants can be put out into the 'no-go' area. An existing nettle patch, however, may need to be contained with a fence, wall or path; or better still, transfer clumps of nettles to large tubs or barrels sunk into the ground to prevent the roots from encroaching into the garden proper. Emerging caterpillars prefer fresh, new leaves to feed on, so cut back half the patch in early or mid-summer to encourage new growth.

HABITAT BOOSTERS

A sheet of corrugated iron does not look very attractive, but if you happen to have one, it is worth keeping. As the sun warms the metal, the 'tunnels' beneath become inviting resting quarters for slow worms and grass snakes. Equally, an old paving slab laid over a hollow in a shady spot makes a damp hiding place for frogs and toads.

'No Go' Area Checklist

- ☐ Log pile
- ☐ Nettle patch
- ☐ Leaf pile
- ☐ Hedgehog box
- ☐ Corrugated iron
- ☐ Old paving slabs

WARNING

Don't allow the 'wild' area to become used as a rubbish dump. Household rubbish such as tin cans and broken bottles can be lethal to hedgehogs, foxes and other mammals who may try to eat or drink the contents, with serious consequences.

BRAMBLES – A THORNY ISSUE

Bramble or wild blackberry (*Rubus fruticosus*) is present in many gardens, and the question is, should gardeners be encouraging it, or should it be ripped out? As a wildlife plant, the bramble has enormous value. The flowers provide pollen for bees and nectar for butterflies all through the summer and it supports a wide range of insects. The berries are a useful food supplement for small mammals and birds. It can be trained as a climber, to cover a wall, and its dense, thorny growth makes excellent cover for nesting birds.

However, it is extremely difficult to control. A bramble thicket becomes impenetrable after a few years and the roots of established bushes are deeply anchored. Removing a bramble requires brute strength and endless patience as the tiniest piece of root left in the soil will spring back to life year after year. It is therfore not a good idea to introduce bramble into a small garden. If bramble already exists, one or two bushes could be retained, cutting out the old wood every other year and removing suckers and seedlings as soon as they appear. In larger gardens, a bramble patch can be accommodated, but will still need to be contained within its allotted space.

PLANNING A NECTAR-RICH FLOWER BORDER

Summer is a good time to plan a new border or to consider making an existing one more attractive to garden wildlife. Providing nectar is essential if you hope to attract butterflies. Hopefully, as different species come in to feed on the flowers they will stay to breed and over-winter in the garden.

It is the scent and colour of flowers that signal to the butterflies that nectar is present. They seem to prefer heavy perfumes, but don't seem to be too fussy about colour. Bees also feed on nectar (as well as collecting pollen to feed their young). Initially they are attracted by the scent and colour, but as they approach the flowers they are guided into the centre by markings on the petals – such as those on foxgloves and pansies – which are more apparent in the bees' ultraviolet vision.

ANNUAL FLOWERS

Candytuft, tobacco plant and marigolds are placed near the front of the border where they can easily be taken out and replaced each year.

There is no need to grow wildflowers exclusively in order to provide nectar. In fact, many of the garden-imported species and varieties are nectar-rich. Spend some time during the summer months studying your own garden and others you visit, making a note of which flowers are most attractive to bees and butterflies. From early autumn, many of the plants should be available as young pot-grown specimens in garden centres and nurseries.

Plant the border in autumn to give the plants a chance to get established before the cold weather comes. By spring, the border should be off to a good start.

FOOD FOR ALL

Each type of flower is designed to attract a different feeder. Those with flat, open flowers (such as roses) where the nectar is fully exposed are the province of flies and beetles. Bumble bees, with their fairly long tongues and hairy bodies, can prise open the flowers of snapdragons and bluebells. Those flowers which keep nectar at the base of a long tube (like red valerian) are only accessible to long-tongued butterflies and moths. However, all creatures are opportunists and will feed on whatever plants are available.

RECOMMENDED PLANTS FOR NECTAR-RICH FLOWER BORDER

PLANT	TYPE/SEASON	WILDLIFE VALUE
BUDDLEIA (*Buddleia davidii*)	Shrub/late summer	Peacocks, whites, small tortoiseshells, commas, red admirals, brimstones
VERBENA (*Verbena bonariensis*)	Perennial/summer to late autumn	Most butterfly species
SEDUM (*Sedum spectabile*)	Perennial/autumn	Most butterfly species – especially small tortoiseshells, bumble bees
CANDYTUFT (*Iberis umbellata*)	Annual/summer	Most butterfly species
YELLOW ALYSSUM (*Alyssum saxatile*)	Perennial/spring	Orange tips, small tortoiseshells, peacocks
FRENCH MARIGOLD (*Tagetes patula*)	Annual/summer to autumn	Most butterfly species
TOBACCO PLANT (*Nicotiana alata*)	Annual/summer	Moths – especially hawkmoths
GOLDEN ROD (*Solidago canadensis*)	Perennial/autumn	Most butterfly species
FLOWERING CURRANT (*Ribes sanguineum*)	Shrub/spring	Bees, early broods of butterflies
HONEYSUCKLE (*Lonicera* spp.)	Climber/summer to autumn	Long-tongued moths, butterflies, bees
GLOBE THISTLE (*Echinops ritro*)	Perennial/summer	Bees
PHLOX (*Phlox paniculata*)	Perennial/summer	Most butterfly species, moths
RED VALERIAN (*Centranthus rubra*)	Perennial/summer to autumn	Hawkmoths, elephant hawkmoths, small tortoiseshells
MICHAELMAS DAISIES (*Aster novi-belgii*)	Perennial/autumn	Small coppers, tortoiseshells
LAVENDER (*Lavendula* spp.)	Shrub/summer to autumn	Meadow browns, late broods of whites, bees

AUGUST

The pleasures of wildlife watching this month are heightened by the good weather. The garden is literally seething with activity as the warmer temperatures bring in greater numbers of hoverflies and ladybirds, both good friends to the wildlife gardener. Hot, humid conditions can trigger an invasion of both insects, who will earn their keep by keeping the greenfly population in check. One hoverfly may look much like another, but in fact around a hundred different species have been recorded in British gardens.

The surface of the pond will also be alive with new generations of darter dragonflies, waterboatmen and pond skaters. Tiny midge-like insects provide food, not only for the dragonflies but also for swifts and swallows who will scoop them up in thousands every day. Bats also make use of these feeding grounds, leaving their roosts at night to hunt for insects. With their young well matured, the females can leave the nursery sites again. Pipistrelles are the most common bats in urban areas, but near canals and rivers the Daubenton's bat is just as likely to be seen racing along the course of the water. In dry spells, the pond and surrounding marsh will be the focus of activity for mammals like hedgehogs and foxes who, exhausted by the heat, may forget their natural timidity and drink at the water's edge in broad daylight.

Some birds can be seen drinking and washing in the pond, but overall this is an unrewarding time of the year for garden bird watching. Although the new broods of young will be boldly exploring their surroundings, the adults are more likely to be lying low in the undergrowth, undergoing their summer moult. Losing feathers makes flight difficult and most species tend to remain quietly hidden, hence the noticeable absence of birdsong.

TASKS FOR THE MONTH

- [ ] *Take semi-hardwood cuttings*
- [ ] *Water containers and berry-bearing shrubs*
- [ ] *Set up pond alternatives*
- [ ] *Trim evergreen hedges*

LAST-MINUTE PLANTING

This is the last chance to plant meadow saffron (*Colchicum autumnale*) and autumn crocus (*Crocus speciosus*) (see tasks for the month of July for planting instructions).

TAKING SEMI-HARDWOOD CUTTINGS

Mid- to late summer is the time to take semi-hardwood cuttings of shrubs like lavender and ceanothus which do not root well from the more usual autumn hardwood cuttings. A semi- hardwood cutting is taken from the current year's growth which has begun to get woody towards the base but is still green and soft at the tip. They take a little more care than the hardwood cuttings, but the trouble is worthwhile for any shrubs that prove difficult to propagate.

- Choose this year's growth (easily identifiable as the shoots with leaves growing on them) and select a side shoot about 15–20cm (6–8in) long. Using secateurs, cut the shoot near to the point where it meets the main stem.

- Using a sharp knife, take off the lower leaves and trim the cutting just below a leaf joint. Take off the soft tip, just above a leaf joint so that the finished cutting is 5–10cm (2–4in) long.

- Insert the cutting to one-third of its length in a small pot of seed or cuttings compost.

SHRUBS FROM WHICH TO TAKE SEMI-HARDWOOD CUTTINGS

Barberry (*Berberis thunbergii*) F

Ceanothus (*C. x burkwoodii*) N

Firethorn (*Pyracantha*) F

Guelder rose (*Viburnum opulus*) F

Honeysuckle (*Lonicera periclymenum*) N

Japanese quince (*Chaenomeles speciosa*) F

Lavender (*Lavandula*) B, N

Rosemary (*Rosmarinus officinalis*) B, N

Shrubby cinquefoil (*Potentilla fruticosa*) B, N

TAKE EXTRA CUTTINGS

As not all cuttings will be successful it is worth taking a few extra cuttings from each shrub.

- Water well with a fine sprayer and cover the pot with a polythene bag, secured with a rubber band. A plastic drinks bottle cut in half and placed over the pot also works well.

- Place the pot in a warm place (16–18°C/61–64°F) but out of direct sunlight. The cuttings should root in two to three weeks.

- Harden off the cuttings by gradually lifting the polythene to allow more air to circulate over the next three to four weeks.

- Transfer the cuttings individually into larger pots. Place the pots in a cool greenhouse or coldframe and keep well watered. Plant outside in the spring.

WATERING

In any hot, dry spells container plants will need to be watered every day to stop them drying out. Pay special attention to hanging baskets and small pots. It is also worth watering berry-bearing shrubs like cotoneaster and pyracantha as lack of moisture can lead to a poor crop in the autumn. Frequent watering will help to swell the developing fruit.

POND ALTERNATIVES

Birds, too, can suffer in particularly dry summers. Check the pond level and top up if necessary. Rainwater is preferable if available from a barrel or waterbutt, as tapwater can lead to the growth of algae in the pond. If the garden does not have a pond, then it is vital to provide alternative wildlife drinking and washing places. Any unwanted shallow kitchen container can be repurposed into a bird's drinking vessel. Even a large terracotta saucer or dish will suffice. Check the levels daily and fill up as necessary.

TRIMMING EVERGREEN HEDGES

Evergreen hedges (single species or mixed) can be clipped now. Overgrown holly, yew, laurel or privet will benefit from a trim, once the danger of disturbing nesting birds is past. Use sharp hedging shears and keep the blades flat against the face of the hedge. Cut the top of the hedge with the shears held horizontally. Long hedges may need a power hedge trimmer.

NATIVE HEDGE CLIPPING
Native hedges do not need clipping every year and should only be clipped to retain shape and control over-exuberant growth.

Plants of the Month

WILD ANGELICA (*Angelica sylvestris*)

Most at home in damp meadows, fens and on river banks, wild angelica is a widely distributed wild herb. The tall stems are distinguished from the more commonly grown garden angelica by their slender growth and purplish-pink colour. Wild angelica has a rather bitter taste but it makes a good architectural plant for the pond edge or marsh.

TYPE Perennial herb

FLOWERS White or pink, summer to autumn

HEIGHT 2m (6ft)

PLANTING Plant in early spring, leaving 1m (3ft) between plants

SITE Sun or partial shade, in marshy ground, by ponds or in damp meadows

SOIL Damp, rich soil

CARE Wild angelica is fairly short-lived, so plants can be discarded and replaced after two to three years

PROPAGATION Self-seeds easily; or collect seed in early autumn, store and sow outdoors in spring

VARIETIES Garden angelica (*Angelica archangelica*) is now widely naturalised and is used to flavour liqueurs. The leaves are dried and used in teas and pot pourri

WILDLIFE Wide, open flowerheads makes angelica accessible to small insects like hoverflies. The seedheads provide useful food for birds in late summer and early autumn

PURPLE LOOSESTRIFE (*Lythium salicaria*)

A native flower of pond edges, marshes and wetlands. The spires of purple flowers are excellent for the wildlife garden, blooming throughout the summer.

TYPE Perennial

FLOWERS Purple, summer

HEIGHT 1m (3ft)

PLANTING Plant young specimens in spring or autumn 45cm (18in) apart

SITE Sun or partial shade at pond edge or wetland

SOIL Moist

CARE Divide roots in autumn if plant has outgrown its space

PROPAGATION Self-seeds easily. May also be grown from purchased seed

WILDLIFE Supplies nectar and pollen for bees and butterflies; caterpillars of the small hawkmoth feed on the leaves

LADY'S BEDSTRAW
(*Galium verum*)

A common wayside flower, found in grass-lands, on sand dunes and road verges. Originally known as 'Our Lady's Bedstraw', it was reputed to have been used to scent the stable bedding in Bethlehem. Traditionally, the sweet-smelling dried flowerheads were added to the straw used to fill mattresses.

TYPE Perennial

FLOWERS Golden yellow, summer

HEIGHT 45cm (18in)

HABIT Sprawling

PLANTING Young pot-grown plants should be put out in autumn

SITE Full sun, in a meadow or border

SOIL Dry, poor

CARE If grown as part of a meadow, the grass should be left uncut until early autumn

PROPAGATION Lady's bedstraw will spread rapidly through a meadow without any intervention. It can also be grown from seed collected in early autumn or bought from a nursery

WILDLIFE A valuable native constituent of the summer-flowering meadow. The strong scent attracts a wide variety of insects, particularly butterflies and hawkmoths

TREE MALLOW
(*Lavatera thuringiaca 'Rosea'*)

A vigorous shrub, often distrusted by gardeners because of its tendency to grow coarse and woody. It grows quickly, even on poor soils, to produce a large, handsome plant bearing masses of pink flowers that last right through the summer and well into autumn.

TYPE Semi-evergreen woody perennial

FLOWERS Rose-pink, mid-summer to late autumn

HEIGHT 1.2m (4ft)

SPREAD 1.2m (4ft)

PLANTING Put out young plants in spring or autumn, 1.2m (4ft) apart

SITE Sun

SOIL Any, well-drained

CARE If plant starts to outgrow its space, cut stems back to ground level in early spring

PROPAGATION From semi-hardwood cuttings in late summer

WILDLIFE Bees, butterflies and flying insects flock to the open flowers which appear continuously for over four months of the year

SEA HOLLY
(*Eryngium maritimum*)

A hardy native perennial found growing on sands, rocks and shingle around the coasts of Britain. The distinctive spiky blue-green leaves and powder-blue flowers make the sea holly a popular border plant.

TYPE Perennial

FLOWERS Blue, mid-summer to early autumn

HEIGHT 45cm (18in)

SPREAD 30cm (12in)

PLANTING Young pot-grown plants should be planted 30cm (12in) apart between autumn and spring

SITE Sun

SOIL Well-drained

CARE Cut stems to ground level in early spring

PROPAGATION Sow seeds in spring

WILDLIFE Bees, beetles and sometimes butterflies seek out the flowerheads for nectar

HAREBELL (*Campanula rotundifolia*)

Known in Scotland as the bluebell, it is in fact a completely different species to the English bluebell (*Scilla non-scripta*). The harebell is a widespread native of sand dunes, grassy banks, heaths and downs and is often cultivated in gardens for its pretty bell-shaped flowers.

TYPE Perennial

FLOWERS Blue, occasionally white, mid- to late summer

HEIGHT 30cm (12in)

PLANTING Plant out pot-grown specimens in early autumn or spring

SITE Sun or partial shade. In flowering meadows, borders, dry-stone walls, rock gardens and containers

SOIL Poor, dry soil preferred but will tolerate normal border soil

CARE If grown in a meadow, wait until early autumn before cutting

PROPAGATION From seed collected in early autumn

RELATED Most of the garden campanula species, although not native, are useful for attracting insects. C. *lactiflora* makes an attractive, tall border plant and C. *carpatica* can be grown on walls and in rock gardens where it forms a compact mat

WILDLIFE Harebells rely on bees for pollination and are attractive to most flying insects. As part of a summer-flowering meadow they will attract many different species of butterfly including small whites

HEATHER (*Calluna vulgaris*)

The heather family (*Ericaceae*) make excellent plants for a wildlife garden, provided the soil is not too limy. The summer-flowering heather or ling (*C. vulgaris*) gives good ground cover to birds, insects and reptiles.

TYPE Sub-shrub

FLOWERS Lilac to pale purple, mid- to late summer

HEIGHT 30–60cm (12–24in)

SPREAD 30–60cm (12–24in)

PLANTING Plant in groups, during spring or in late autumn. Space the plants 45cm (18in) apart. Make sure the roots are buried deeply and the foliage rests on the soil surface. Water after planting and during any dry spells for the first year of growth

SITE Open, sunny site in borders, rock gardens or containers

SOIL Prefers a peat-based, acid soil. If the soil tends towards lime, it is best not to try to grow heathers, and not add peat artificially

CARE Mulching around the roots will prevent water loss. The flowerheads can be left on the plants through the winter and clipped off in the spring to encourage new growth

PROPAGATION By semi-hardwood cuttings taken in late summer

WILDLIFE The spreading, low-growing mounds offer protection to ground-feeding birds like wrens and the insects they are seeking. Grass snakes and slow worms may seek out the sun-soaked patches between the plants, where they are safe from human feet

GLOBE THISTLE (*Echinops ritro*)

Originating from southern Europe, the globe thistle has long been cultivated in British gardens. The thistle-like leaves are in fact downy underneath and not at all prickly. The globe-shaped, steel blue flowerheads make this an attractive border plant with the added bonus that bees seem to love it.

TYPE Perennial

FLOWERS Blue, late summer, early autumn

HEIGHT 1–1.2m (3–4ft)

PLANTING Set out young plants in autumn or spring, 60cm (24in) apart

SITE Sunny, in borders

SOIL Well-drained

CARE Cut back stems to ground level in spring to make room for new growth. (Leave the seedheads intact through autumn and winter)

PROPAGATION Lift and divide plants in autumn or spring

WILDLIFE Bumble bees and many species of butterfly seem to enjoy extracting the nectar from the short tubular flowers. The seedheads are popular with finches in autumn and winter

PLANNING A HERB BED OR GARDEN

Herbs have been part of cultivated gardens for over two thousand years. Many of our most familiar herbs were introduced into the country at some point in history, but have been with us so long that to say they are not native is rather academic. Certainly many garden escapees have become naturalised and have adopted the countryside as their own. However purist we may be about using native plants, few gardeners would banish herbs from the garden. Not only have they a proven use in cooking and health treatments, but they are extremely decorative and blend in well with a natural-looking garden.

RECOMMENDED TOP HERBS FOR WILDLIFE

HERB	TYPE	WILDLIFE VALUE
ANGELICA (*Angelica archangelica*)	Biennial	Flowers – hoverflies, bees Leaves – butterflies, caterpillars Seedheads – greenfinches, blue tits
BORAGE (*Borago officinalis*) Nat	Annual	Flowers – bees
CHIVES (*Allium schoenoprasum*) Nat	Perennial	Flowers – bees, butterflies
COMFREY (*Symphytum uplandicum*) Nat	Perennial	Leaves – moths, butterflies
FENNEL (*Foeniculum vulgare*) Nat	Perennial	Flowers – bees, wasps, hoverflies Leaves – caterpillars
HYSSOP (*Hyssopus officinalis*) Nat	Perennial	Flowers – lacewings, bees
LAVENDER (*Lavandula angustifolia*)	Shrub	Flowers – bees, butterflies
MARJORAM (*Origanum vulgare*) Nat	Perennial	Flowers – bees, butterflies
MINT (*Mentha* – all types) Nat	Perennial	Flowers – bees, butterflies, moths
ROSEMARY (*Rosmarinus officinalis*)	Shrub	Flowers – bees, butterflies, hoverflies
THYME (*Thymus* – all types) Nat	Perennial/ small shrub	Flowers – bees, butterflies

PREPARING THE SITE

The best location for a herb bed is one which gets a lot of sun and where the soil is already well drained. Most herbs dislike getting waterlogged roots and can tolerate almost drought conditions – in fact, those like rosemary and marjoram with Mediterranean ancestry improve in taste, scent and flower growth in a sunny location.

• If the soil is not ideal (heavy clay for instance), it is possible to add some coarse grit to aid drainage. However, it might be simpler and more productive to grow the herbs in pots, putting in a good layer of gravel before adding the compost.

• The ground should be dug thoroughly, removing any weeds and large stones. Lay brick paths, edging tiles or wooden dividers before planting the herbs.

PLANNING THE HERB GARDEN

For human requirements, it is useful to have all the herbs grouped together within easy reach of the kitchen or back door. Wildlife, on the other hand, will happily seek out their favourite herbs wherever they are planted. If it is not practical to make a special herb bed, individual plants can be incorporated into the general garden planting. Thyme, for example, grows well over an old stone wall and rosemary could be included in a sunny shrub border. If space is limited, one solution might be to plant the herbs in pots, window boxes or troughs. However, if there is room, it is very satisfying to devote a special part of the garden to herb growing. This can be any shape at all: linear rows (like a vegetable plot) perhaps divided by a lavender hedge; a circle divided into segments to keep the different species apart; a rectangular plot intersected by paths to allow easy maintenance; or a more ambitious knot garden, marked out with clipped box edging.

A HERB WHEEL

THYME

EAU-DE-COLOGNE MINT

CHIVES

LEMON BALM

BORAGE

SPEARMINT

PEPPERMINT

MARJORAM

THYME

PARSLEY

APPLEMINT

*MINT
The four different varieties of mint are contained in narrow segments to prevent them over-running the entire bed.*

LEAVE HERBS TO FLOWER

Herbs that are grown primarily for their leaves, either for cooking or medicine, usually have their flowerheads removed to encourage consistent leaf growth. Instead of snipping off the flowers as they appear, leave a few plants of parsley, mint, marjoram and lemon balm to flower naturally. Many more insects will visit the plants and consequently the herb garden will be a richer feeding ground for birds.

PLANTING AND MAINTENANCE CALENDAR

LATE SUMMER Prepare site

AUTUMN Plant shrubs and pot-grown perennials

SPRING Sow seeds of annuals

LATE SPRING Sow seeds of biennials

SUMMER Keep beds free of weeds; water container plants

RECTANGULAR PLOT INTERSECTED BY PATHS

FENNEL   CHIVES   THYME   LAVENDER   HYSSOP   MAJORAM   ROSEMARY

BUTTERFLY NECTAR

The flowers of herbs such as hyssop, lavender, catmint, marjoram and thyme are useful sources of nectar for summer butterflies.

HERBS FOR LESS-THAN-IDEAL CONDITIONS

Although most herbs prefer a sunny position in a well-drained soil, there are some which will tolerate shade and a heavier soil. The resulting plants may not do as well but there is no need to give up the idea of growing herbs altogether and the wildlife will still find them useful.

Mint (*Mentha*) can tolerate shade although it does tend to grow towards the light and become crooked and leggy.

Tansy (*Tanacetum vulgare*) is an excellent native plant for butterflies and it is not too fussy about growing conditions.

Lovage (*Levisticum officinale*), a relative of the fennel, is also worth growing for its young leaves which add a celery flavour to soups and stews. It will grow quite adequately in a dark, damp spot and the flowers produced, although not as abundant as they should be, will provide nectar for hoverflies, wasps and bees.

Comfrey (*Symphytum* x *uplandicum*) should be included purely for its leaves which are a reliable food source for moth and butterfly caterpillars.

Lemon balm (*Melissa officinalis*) is another strong grower in less than ideal conditions. Its white or pale yellow flowers rely on bees for their pollination.

Garden chervil (*Anthriscus cerefolium*) is an annual herb, greatly prized for the flavour of its parsley-like leaves. It will tolerate some shade, but prefers a well-drained soil.

SEEDS FOR THE BIRDS
Chicory, angelica, lovage and fennel all provide an accessible supply of bird seed after they have finished flowering.

Great burnet (*Sanguisorba officinalis*) is a tall native herb that prefers a damp habitat and a heavy clay soil. The tiny crimson flowers appear from mid-summer through to early autumn.

Angelica (*Angelica archangelica*), originally from central Europe, is widely naturalised in Britain. It will do well in a shady spot in damp soil and has huge seedheads in early autumn.

TRADITIONAL HERB GARDEN LAYOUTS
PATHS MAY BE PAVING, GRASS, BRICKS OR GRAVEL

STONE BIRDBATH
*UNDERPLANTED WITH LOW-GROWING
HERB SEGMENTS DIVIDED BY STONES*

LOW-GROWING HERBS

Choose low-growing herbs:
thyme, chives, dwarf lavender
and marjoram.

SEPTEMBER

This part of the year, when summer draws to a close and moves ever closer to autumn, is one of the most enjoyable times in the wildlife garden calendar. All of the bird species should be more in evidence after their late summer moult, and birdsong fills the air once more. The days are still warm, and long enough for the gardener to stay outside until dusk, when bats can often be seen circling overhead, catching insects in flight.

There should still be dragonflies dancing over any marshy areas or ponds and this is a good time for butterfly watching, as the third generation of adults emerge to take advantage of the late summer flowers. In woodland areas, the speckled wood butterfly may also be seen fluttering in the dappled sunlight.

In the bird kingdom, this is the start of the outward migration period, clearing the airways for the influx of continental visitors due next month. Swifts and swallows announce their departure south with aerial displays of divebombing, accompanied by loud screeching. Their close cousins, the housemartins, seem more reluctant to leave and often hang on for another month or two. Other species starting to depart now include the garden and willow warblers, blackcaps and pied flycatchers.

Native hedgerows are bursting with hips and berries, making rewarding hunting grounds for moths, insects, birds and small mammals. The wild blackberry, or bramble, is also at its peak, bearing luscious edible fruits, but it is planted at the gardener's peril. It is a matter of weighing up the hours of backbreaking work needed to dig out the bushes when they inevitably begin to take over, against the undoubted wildlife benefits of the fruit, flowers and thorny stems which give such good protection to nesting birds.

TASKS FOR THE MONTH

- [ ] *Last cut for the meadow/wildflower lawn*
- [ ] *Harvest fruit*
- [ ] *Plant evergreen shrubs and trees*
- [ ] *Clear annual flower beds*
- [ ] *Collect seed*

FINAL MOWING OF THE WILDFLOWER LAWN

Lawns or meadows that have been left uncut to allow later flowering species to develop can be mown now. Use a rotary mower, heavy duty strimmer or a hand scythe and cut the grass to leave 8cm (3in) of stubble (strimmers and scythes can be extremely dangerous if handled incorrectly; if in doubt, get help from someone who is experienced in the use of agricultural tools). Leave the cuttings on the ground for a day or two to allow insects to find their way back to ground, then rake them off and add to the compost heap.

THE FRUIT HARVEST

Traditional gardeners are gathering in the harvest of fruits and vegetables now, eating some and storing the rest away for use later in the winter. Try leaving some plums and pears on the tree where, as they soften and become more juicy, they will attract butterflies galore. Instead of taking all the apple crop indoors for storage, leave at least half the fruit intact to provide on-tree and windfallen fare for hungry birds. Some of the stored crop can be kept until mid-winter, when it can be strewn on the lawn to attract visiting redwings.

USING EVERGREEN SHRUBS AND TREES

The ubiquitous conifer has been so overused in conventional gardens that wildlife gardeners tend to treat all evergreens with disdain. Yet, a carefully chosen selection of evergreen trees and shrubs can provide some unexpected benefits for wildlife, not to mention an important structural component of the garden. The yew, Scots pine and holly are all native evergreens well worth including if space allows, while ornamental shrubs like viburnums, mahonias and the evergreen cotoneasters carry useful flowers and berries which add to the food stock available to wildlife.

BUTTERFLY BUSHES

Snip off the faded flowers of buddleia bushes now to encourage them to keep on flowering. Many butterfly species will visit the bush well into the autumn.

PLANTING EVERGREEN SHRUBS

· Dig a hole as deep as, and slightly wider than, the shrub's container. Loosen the soil at the bottom of the hole with a fork and add a handful of garden compost.

· Place the shrub in the hole, checking that the soil will cover it to the same depth as it did in the container (bare-root plants should have a soil mark on the stem).

· Fill the hole with loose soil, tread down firmly and add more soil if necessary. Tread the soil down again.

· Water the soil around the shrub thoroughly so that it soaks right down to the roots.

USEFUL EVERGREENS

NAME	WILDLIFE VALUE
COTONEASTER (*C. dammeri, C. simonsii, C. microphyllus*)	Abundant berries
FIRETHORN (*Pyracantha* – species and hybrids)	Winter berries and spring flowers
HOLLY (*Ilex aquifolium*) Nat	Secure nesting and berries
OREGON GRAPE (*Mahonia aquifolium*)	Early flowers for nectar and autumn berries
SCOTS PINE (*Pinus sylvestris*) Nat	Crossbills prise the seed from pine cones
VIBURNUM (*Viburnum tinus*)	Early flowers for nectar
YEW (*Taxus baccata*) Nat	Makes an excellent nesting hedge

TALL TREES

If grown as a tree rather than a hedge, yew can reach 20m (65ft) and Scots pine frequently 40m (130ft), so these species should only be considered for large gardens. They can be planted this month and planting instructions are as for deciduous trees (see the practical project for October).

CLEARING ANNUAL FLOWER BEDS

Many annual flowers are coming to the end of their life and the space may be needed for other plants. The most common procedure at this stage is to clear the flower beds completely and deposit the dying plants on the compost heap. However, there are some annuals, like sunflowers, that produce seed which the birds love. If the bed must be cleared, a good compromise is to cut off the seedheads first, tie them in a bunch and hang them from a windowsill, fence or from a low branch away from cats, where they will still be accessible to greenfinches and other seed eaters.

COLLECTING SEED

Annual seed can also be collected now for sowing next year. Snip off entire seedheads and place them upside down in a paper bag. If the seeds are ripe, a few shakes of the bag should dislodge them. Spread the contents of the bag onto a tray and separate out the seeds. Pour into airtight containers, and don't forget to label them before storing in a cool, dark place until spring. Some seeds including larkspur and poppy - are poisonous, so take care when handling and keep away from children and pets. If in doubt, check with the Royal Horticultural Society (see Resources).

Seed may also be collected from perennials to increase your stock of wildlife plants for borders, meadow and wetland. Ragged robin, greater knapweed, lady's bedstraw and field scabious can all be propagated from seed.

FLOWERS FOR SEED COLLECTION

Corncockle (Agrostemma githago)

Evening primrose (Oenothera biennis)

Larkspur (Delphinium consolida)

Night-scented stock (Matthiola bicornis)

Poppy (Papaver rhoeas)

Teasel (Dipsacus fullonum)

Sunflower (Helianthus annuus)

TESTING FOR RIPENESS

Seeds are 'ripe' when they come away freely from the flowerhead, after the flower has faded. If the seeds do not shake free easily, put the heads into a paper bag then hang them in a dry place for a period of up to two weeks, until the seeds fall naturally to the bottom of the bag.

Plants of the Month

ELDER (*Sambucus nigra*)

The native elder grows prodigiously on waste and scrublands, in woods and on riverbanks. People and wildlife compete for its favours, as both flowers and fruit are used in winemaking and the fruit is particularly rich in vitamin C.

TYPE Deciduous shrub or small tree

FLOWERS Creamy white, mid-summer

FRUITS Black berries, early autumn

HEIGHT To 4m (13ft)

SPREAD 3.6m (12ft)

PLANTING Plant young trees between mid-autumn and early spring

SITE Sun or partial shade. Can be part of a mixed hedge, shrubbery or woodland edge

SOIL Fertile

CARE No pruning necessary. Elder can be coppiced in winter but no flowers or berries will be produced the following year

PROPAGATION Take hardwood cuttings in mid-autumn for planting out a year later

VARIETIES The golden elder, *S. nigra* 'Aurea', is worth growing for the golden colour of the young leaves

WILDLIFE Mainly grown for its rich crop of berries which are amongst the first shrub or hedgerow fruits to ripen. Most of the resident garden birds will feast on the berry-laden branches. The summer flowers are also a useful nectar source for insects

GOLDEN ROD (*Solidago canadensis*)

Introduced from North America and now widely naturalised, golden rod is now also a popular garden plant. It is one of the essential components of a traditional herbaceous border. The smaller, native golden rod (*S. virgaurea*) flowers earlier and is not as well known, although seed can be obtained from some wildflower nurseries.

TYPE Perennial

FLOWERS Yellow plumes, late summer to mid-autumn

HEIGHT 1–1.5m (3–5ft)

SPREAD 1m (3ft)

PLANTING Plant between mid-autumn and early spring, 60cm (2ft) apart

SITE Sun or partial shade, in borders

SOIL Any

CARE No special care needed. Tall plants may need staking

PROPAGATION Divide plants in autumn or late winter, or grow from seeds sown in spring. Golden rod also self-seeds very readily

VARIETIES Hundreds of varieties are available derived from *S. canadensis* and *S. virgaurea*. 'Golden Thumb' is a good dwarf variety, 30cm (12in) high. Other full-size varieties worth growing are 'Golden Gates' and 'Cloth of Gold'

WILDLIFE Very attractive to moths, as well as a wide range of other insect species. The fluffy seedheads later in the autumn are particularly relished by seed-eating birds

SEDUM (*Sedum spectabile*)

Sedum spectabile is
an exotic member of
the stonecrop family
which, as the name
suggests, inhabits rocky
locations in many areas.
The garden sedums,
however, can be grown
in any ordinary soil and
are some of the best wildlife plants for the
flower border.

TYPE Perennial

FLOWERS Pink, crimson or mauve, autumn

HEIGHT 30–45cm (12–18in)

PLANTING Plant between autumn and
early spring, 45cm (18in) apart

SITE Full sun in borders, rock gardens or
containers

SOIL Well-drained

CARE Sedums are resistant to drought so
should not need extra watering

PROPAGATION Divide and replant between
mid-autumn and early spring

VARIETIES 'Autumn Joy' is a delicate,
salmon-pink; 'Brilliant' is a stronger shade

WILDLIFE Small tortoiseshell butterflies
flock to sedum, as do most insects in
search of nectar. The wide flowerheads
remain intact into late autumn, when most
flowers in the border have run to seed

TEASEL (*Dipsacus fullonum*)

The wild teasel makes a
good garden border plant,
establishing itself in many
different kinds of habitat
and providing a wide
range of wildlife interest.
The closely related Fuller's
teasel (*D. fullonum* subsp.
sativus) is still cultivated
commercially for its hard spiky seedheads which
are used to raise the nap of fine worsted cloth in
traditional weaving mills.

TYPE Biennial

FLOWERS Pink/purple, mid-summer

SEEDHEADS Brown, spiny, early autumn

HEIGHT To 2m (6½ft)

PLANTING Plant out small pot-grown plants in
mid-autumn

SITE Open, sunny position in borders

SOIL Any

CARE No special care needed

PROPAGATION By seed collected in autumn
and sown in spring. As teasel is biennial, the
spikes will not appear until the second year. It
self-seeds quite readily

WILDLIFE The huge, honeycombed seedheads
will be flocked by goldfinches each autumn,
teasing out the seed with their beaks. Earlier
in the year the bracts around the stem form a
reservoir, which attracts insects and small birds
to drink the collected rainwater. Although the
flowers are short-lived, they attract bees and a
good range of butterflies, including the common
blue and small copper

SEPTEMBER

CREATING A SUMMER-FLOWERING MEADOW

This is the best time of year to think about making a wildflower meadow to flower next summer. By sowing seeds now, they will have the best chance of becoming established through the autumn and winter. Wildflower seeds can either be sown on bare ground, or incorporated into an existing lawn.

SOWING A WILDFLOWER LAWN

CHOOSING THE SITE

Many wildlife gardeners prefer to keep some of the grassy areas of their garden as conventional lawn and it makes sense to mow the grass closest to the house. A wildflower meadow could be created in any other part of the garden, perhaps beyond the short grass or bordering a woodland area. Choose an area that has not been heavily fertilised – a vegetable patch would not be suitable, but a neglected lawn which has received no feeding or chemicals would be. It is best to avoid sites with a history of persistent weeds like docks and thistles. Choose a sunny location, away from too many overhanging trees.

GROUND PREPARATION

Ground preparation is probably the most important part of the whole operation. Meadow flowers and grasses will only establish themselves on ground with low fertility, so this needs to be given some consideration. One way of reducing soil fertility is to remove the top layer of turf, and possibly the topsoil as well. Dig over thoroughly or cover the area for a complete season with black polythene to ensure all perennial weeds are eradicated.

CHOOSING A SEED MIXTURE

For most situations, a standard meadow mixture containing 20% flower seed and 80% grass seed will be adequate. A typical summer-flowering meadow mixture might include musk mallow, bird's foot trefoil, knapweed and lady's bedstraw, along with a selection of bent and fescue grasses. Good seed merchants will list the exact proportions of all the constituents of their mixtures. There is also a range of mixtures designed specifically for unusual growing conditions such as particularly sandy or chalky soils or damp, marshy ground.

The meadow mixture can either be sown alone or mixed with some annual cornfield flower seeds. This is termed 'nursing' and, although it is not strictly necessary, the annuals will provide cover for the developing perennials, which take longer to establish. This method has the added advantage of giving a bright display of poppies and cornflowers in the first year.

SOWING THE SEED

1. Remove all large stones from the earth and rake it thoroughly. Sieve the soil through a large garden sieve if necessary, to produce a fine tilth. Continue raking and treading the surface until it is absolutely level.

2. Water the ground with a sprinkler hose or a watering-can with a fine rose until soaked.

3. Mix together the meadow and annual seeds (if used). Sow the seed thinly – a rough guide is 4gm per square metre (⅛oz per 10 square feet), but check the instructions for each particular mixture. To ensure an even coverage, walk the plot in one direction, sowing at only half the recommended rate. Then walk the plot in the opposite direction, sowing the remainder of the seed. The seed can be broadcast by hand and it will be easier to spread if mixed with a little silver sand before sowing.

PLAN FOR THE SITE OF A WILDFLOWER MEADOW

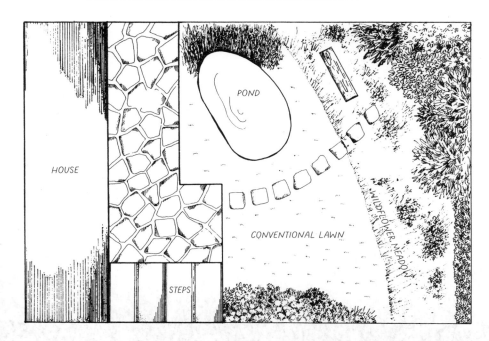

AFTERCARE IN THE FIRST YEAR

Meadow mixture only Make the first cut when the grass is over 10cm (4in) high (usually about six weeks from the start of the spring growing season). Then cut monthly or as often as necessary to keep the site tidy. On poor soils there may not be much growth and only occasional cutting will be necessary. Remove the cuttings to prevent an increase in fertility.

Meadow mixture sown with cornfield annuals Cut the grass once only, in late summer, after the annuals have flowered. Remove the cuttings after mowing.

MAINTENANCE IN LATER YEARS

The traditional rhythm of meadow maintenance, still practised by a few farmers, is quite straightforward: an annual cut of the meadows in late summer for hay, followed by grazing of livestock through the autumn and winter. This sort of seasonal pattern works just as well for a wildflower lawn, cutting the grass once after the summer display. As far as winter grazing is concerned, mowing occasionally through the autumn and winter will achieve a similar effect. However, it is quite simple to vary the peak flowering period by changing the mowing regime – an earlier cut will encourage more spring-flowering species like cowslips and fritillaries, whilst a later cut benefits the late-flowering knapweeds and field scabious.

INCORPORATING WILDFLOWERS INTO AN EXISTING LAWN

There are basically two ways of doing this, both of which can be implemented in early autumn. The first involves sowing seed, the second planting pot-grown plants. Whichever method is chosen, the best results will be obtained with a lawn that is already patchy and weak in growth. The lush green grass of a well-fed lawn is likely to swamp any wildflowers that are introduced.

SOWING WILDFLOWER SEED

Begin by giving the lawn a thorough raking with a metal rake to remove moss, dead grass and leaves. Water thoroughly and sow the seeds at the manufacturer's recommended rate.

ADDING POT-GROWN WILDFLOWERS

After the last cut of the season is a good time to put in pot-grown wildflowers. More and more nurseries are stocking wildflowers in pots, but remember to choose species that will suit your intended regime of meadow maintenance. Place the plants in groups, with individual plants 20–40cm (8–16in) apart. Remove a plug of earth the same size as the pot, using a bulb planter or trowel. Knock the plants from their pots and place them in the holes, firming down the soil and watering well afterwards.

POT-GROWN WILDFLOWER

PLUG OF SOIL

BULB PLANTER

MEADOW MIXTURE

20% flowering native perennials (see Spring-flowering and Summer-flowering Meadow Perennials)

40% crested dog-tail (native grass)

30% fescue (non-native grass)

10% bent (lawn grass)

SPRING-FLOWERING MEADOW PERENNIALS

Bladder campion (*Silene vulgaris*)

Cowslip (*Primula veris*)

Lady's bedstraw (*Galium verum*)

Meadow buttercup (*Ranunculus acris*)

SUMMER-FLOWERING MEADOW PERENNIALS

Betony (*Stachys officinalis*)

Bird's foot trefoil (*Lotus corniculatus*)

Field scabious (*Knautia arvensis*)

Greater knapweed (*Centaurea scabiosa*)

Meadow cranesbill (*Geranium pratense*)

Musk mallow (*Malva moschata*)

Ox-eye daisy (*Leucanthemum vulgare*)

Rough hawkbit (*Leontodon hispidus*)

Selfheal (*Prunella vulgaris*)

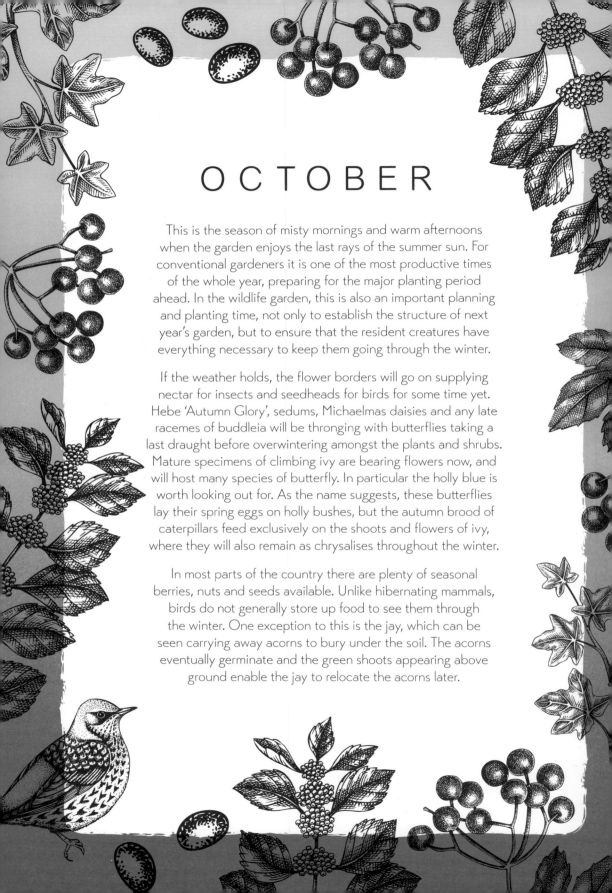

OCTOBER

This is the season of misty mornings and warm afternoons when the garden enjoys the last rays of the summer sun. For conventional gardeners it is one of the most productive times of the whole year, preparing for the major planting period ahead. In the wildlife garden, this is also an important planning and planting time, not only to establish the structure of next year's garden, but to ensure that the resident creatures have everything necessary to keep them going through the winter.

If the weather holds, the flower borders will go on supplying nectar for insects and seedheads for birds for some time yet. Hebe 'Autumn Glory', sedums, Michaelmas daisies and any late racemes of buddleia will be thronging with butterflies taking a last draught before overwintering amongst the plants and shrubs. Mature specimens of climbing ivy are bearing flowers now, and will host many species of butterfly. In particular the holly blue is worth looking out for. As the name suggests, these butterflies lay their spring eggs on holly bushes, but the autumn brood of caterpillars feed exclusively on the shoots and flowers of ivy, where they will also remain as chrysalises throughout the winter.

In most parts of the country there are plenty of seasonal berries, nuts and seeds available. Unlike hibernating mammals, birds do not generally store up food to see them through the winter. One exception to this is the jay, which can be seen carrying away acorns to bury under the soil. The acorns eventually germinate and the green shoots appearing above ground enable the jay to relocate the acorns later.

TASKS FOR THE MONTH

- ☐ Plant out biennials and perennials
- ☐ Plant spring-flowering bulbs
- ☐ Mulch beds and borders
- ☐ Take hardwood cuttings
- ☐ Sow tree and shrub seeds

PLANTING OUT BIENNIALS AND PERENNIALS

This is a good month to put in some of next year's border flowers, particularly any that have been grown from seed in the spring.

Biennial wallflowers, sweet william and foxgloves are tried and trusted cottage-garden flowers that will make a big contribution to the reservoir of nectar, pollen and seed in the coming spring and summer. Container-grown border perennials such as globe thistle, sedum, Michaelmas daisies and hellebores are also good for wildlife and may be planted now.

These plants can be left until spring if you prefer, but an autumn planting will give the roots a good chance of establishing before the cold weather comes. Follow Planting Steps for the best results.

Planting steps

1. Choose the site according to each plant's soil and light requirements.

2. Ensure the soil is in a workable condition – turn over with a fork or add garden compost to improve fertility if necessary.

3. Tap the plants out of their pots. Make a hole with a trowel or spade, slightly bigger than the root ball.

4. Place the plant in the hole, making sure the bottom of the stem is level with the soil in the bed.

5. Fill around the roots with loose soil and firm in.

SPACE TO GROW

Bear in mind that these plants may be only a fraction of their full-grown size. Check the size of each species and allow enough room for plants to grow – plants put in too close together will compete for air, sunlight and nutrients and may develop poorly as a result.

OCTOBER BULB PLANTING

The majority of spring-flowering bulbs can be planted now, although one or two are better left until next month (see tasks for the month of November). Bulbs are one of the easiest ways to ensure a good supply of late winter and spring flowers, providing early nectar for insects, bees and butterflies. The bulbs chosen may be a mixture of native and exotic varieties and, according to type, may be planted in lawns and grassy banks, in flower beds and containers, or under hedgerows and trees. Bulbs look best growing in natural drifts and this effect can be achieved by throwing a handful of bulbs onto the ground and planting them where they fall. If planting in grass, use a specially designed bulb planter (in earth, a trowel works better) to remove a plug of soil. The hole should be approximately twice as deep as the bulb itself. Insert the bulb in the hole, point upwards. Replace the plug of earth and firm in. Note that newly planted bulbs, particularly wild varieties, may take two to three years to get established and flower freely.

RECOMMENDED BULBS

NAME	SITE	PLANTING DEPTH
BLUEBELL (*Scilla non-scripta*) Nat, B, N	Hedgerows, woodland	5cm (2in)
CROCUS (PURPLE) (*Crocus tomasinianus*) N	Lawns, borders, under deciduous trees	8cm (3in)
CROCUS (YELLOW) (*Crocus chrysanthus*) N	Lawns, borders, under deciduous trees	8cm (3in)
GRAPE HYACINTH (*Muscari neglectum*) Nat, B, N	Lawns, borders	8cm (3in)
RAMSONS GARLIC (*Allium ursinum*) Nat, N	Hedgerows, woodland	8cm (3in)
SNOWDROP (*Galanthus nivalis*) Nat	Under deciduous trees, shady borders	5cm (2in)
WILD DAFFODIL (*Narcissus pseudonarcissus*) Nat, B	Lawns, banks	8cm (3in)
WINTER ACONITE (*Eranthis hyemalis*) Nat	Under deciduous trees, shady borders	5cm (2in)

Planting depth = depth of soil *above* the bulb

AUTUMN MULCHING

Permanent shrub or herbaceous borders will benefit from a mulch (a shallow top layer) of garden compost or well-rotted manure. A layer of organic matter can also be spread over empty beds, where it will improve the soil and keep the area weed free until it is replanted. The autumn rains help to take nutrients down into the soil and the extra material will boost the wildlife habitat at ground level, increasing the insect population and making the borders a good feeding ground for birds.

TAKING HARDWOOD CUTTINGS

The simplest way of propagating most deciduous shrubs and trees is by hardwood cuttings, taken when the plants are just starting their period of winter dormancy. Take several cuttings at the same time, from different shrubs, and prepare a nursery bed where they can grow on undisturbed for twelve months. Choose a sheltered site, and dig over thoroughly, removing any weeds and stones.

PLANTS FROM WHICH TO TAKE HARDWOOD CUTTINGS

Broom (*Cytisus scoparius*)

Flowering currant (*Ribes sanguineum*)

Honeysuckle (*Lonicera periclymenum*)

Elder (*Sambucus nigra*)

Ivy (*Hedera helix*)

Wild privet (*Ligustrum ovalifolium*)

Willow (*Salix* spp.)

PROPAGATING TREES AND SHRUBS

Seeds or cuttings? Taking hard and softwood cuttings is certainly the easiest and most reliable way to increase your stock, but the resulting plants will be identical to the parents. In the wild, trees and shrubs spring up naturally from seed and contain a great deal of interesting genetic variation. It is worth having a go at collecting seed, just to see what turns up.

Taking the cuttings

Look for vigorous stems that have just completed a season of growth. They will be hard and woody, with healthy buds all along the length of the stem.

- Using sharp secateurs, cut the stem from the plant near the point where it joins the main branch or stem.

- Using a sharp knife, trim the cutting to 25–30cm (10–12in), cutting just below a bud or leaf joint at the bottom, and just above a bud or leaf joint at the top.

- To encourage rooting, cut away a thin piece of bark from one side of the base.

Planting the cuttings

- Make a trench in the prepared ground by pushing in a spade and pulling it forwards several centimetres (a few inches)–, to form a narrow, v-shaped trench.

- Put a 3–5cm (1¼–2in) layer of coarse sand at the bottom to ensure good drainage. Place the cuttings on the sand so that half to two-thirds of the cutting will be below ground level. Set the cuttings 8–10cm (3–4in) apart. Fill the trench with soil and firm down.

Aftercare

The cuttings should not be disturbed for a full twelve months. If cuttings are 'lifted' by the frost, push them down again gently, so that the base is once again in contact with the sand at the bottom of the trench. Watering will only be needed in particularly dry spells – most likely in the summer months. Keep the area weed free.

By the following autumn, the cuttings should have rooted and have a few sets of leaves. These can be lifted and transplanted to their permanent positions in the garden. If space is limited, they may be put into adequate-sized pots and grown on for one or two years. Any cuttings that have not rooted should be left in position for another year.

GROWING TREES AND SHRUBS FROM SEED

Autumn is the best time to collect tree seeds and berries for propagation. Growing from seed can sometimes be a slow and erratic process, but it is very rewarding in terms of the variety of seedlings produced. Rowan, alder, hazel, elder, shrub roses, hawthorn, guelder rose, blackthorn and most native trees can be grown in this way.

Collecting the seed

Seed should be collected as soon as it is ripe and sown immediately. Seeds which are contained within fleshy fruits, such as rosehips and elderberries, should be squeezed out of their soft casing before sowing. (Note that the seeds of many of these berry-bearing shrubs and trees will only germinate in the wild when they have been eaten, digested and deposited by birds or mammals.)

LEAVE WINDFALL APPLES

Don't collect all the windfallen apples for eating or storing. Leave them on the ground instead where the soft fruit will attract ground-feeding birds species such as the blackbird, as well as providing a late source of energy for butterflies before they overwinter amongst the garden foliage.

Stratification

Many seeds have a hard outer coating which will prevent germination unless it is broken down by any one of the methods known generally as stratification. The simplest way of doing this is to expose the seeds to a period of intense cold which will break down the protective layer. Any seeds which prove difficult to germinate should be sown and the pots left outside for the winter, in a position which is exposed to the action of ice and frost.

Alternatively, the outer coating of large seeds can be damaged by making a little cut in each seed with a sharp penknife. For smaller seeds, rub them between two sheets of sandpaper.

Sowing the seed

Individual seeds should be put into 15cm (6in) pots of proprietary seed compost or a sandy soil, so they lie 2.5cm (1in) beneath the surface of the compost. Stand the pots in a coldframe or cool greenhouse until the following spring. (Most species will germinate in this way, but any that prove difficult should be exposed to frost, as described in Stratification.) As soon as the seeds show signs of growth in the spring, move the pots out into a partially shaded place in the garden. (The seedlings need plenty of light, but should not be exposed to direct sunlight, particularly in the summer months.) Keep the compost moist and grow on, transplanting to bigger pots as necessary. Young trees should be planted out into their permanent positions in autumn, two years after sowing.

COLLECTING SEEDS FROM NUTS, HIPS AND BERRIES

Alder (*Alnus glutinosa*)
Hard, green clusters. These should be collected before they turn brown and woody

Blackthorn (*Prunus spinosa*)
Blue-black, downy fruit. Squeeze flesh to remove seed

Elder (*Sambucus nigra*)
Black berries. Squeeze to remove seed

Guelder rose (*Viburnum opulus*)
Bright red berries. Squeeze to remove seed

Hawthorn
(*Crataegus monogyna*)
Dull red berries. Each berry contains only one seed

Hazel (*Corylus avellana*)
Hard cobnuts. They are ripe for collecting when they change from green to brown

Rowan (*Sorbus aucuparia*)
Red berries. Squeeze fruit to remove seed

Shrub roses (*Rosa* spp.)
Rosehips. Mash to a pulp and leave to dry before extracting

BE PATIENT

Some trees take several years to germinate successfully (particularly if there is not a sufficiently cold 'snap' in winter). So be patient and keep the pots outdoors for two to three seasons before discarding them.

Plants of the Month

IVY (*Hedera helix*)

The common ivy is a hardy climber and one of the real stalwarts of the garden. It is a native plant and can also be found growing widely in woodlands, hedgerows or clambering up the walls of disused buildings. It is a better choice for the wildlife garden than the Canary Island ivy (*H. canariensis*), which is often sold in garden centres. Although a good strong climber, *H. canariensis* does not attract the same range of insects.

TYPE Evergreen climber

HABIT Self-clinging, climbing or trailing

FLOWERS Yellow-green, autumn

FRUITS Green berries, turning black when ripe in mid-winter

HEIGHT Up to 30m (100ft)

PLANTING Put in young plants between early autumn and early spring. (Container-grown plants may be planted at any time of the year.) Water well during first few months, particularly if grown against a wall or in poor soil

SITE Partial or full shade, against fences and walls, on trellises or up old trees, as ground cover or in pots. Prefers some shade, especially from the mid-summer sun, but will in fact tolerate most situations

SOIL Any

CARE No special care needed. Ivies grown against the house may need to be cut back to avoid gutters and windows – do this in early winter, after flowering and before nesting birds move in

PROPAGATION From cuttings taken in autumn

VARIETIES There are hundreds of named varieties and as far as wildlife is concerned it does not really matter which are grown

WILDLIFE Flowers produce a supply of nectar throughout the autumn and will be visited by hoverflies, holly blue and tortoiseshell butterflies. As winter comes, the leaves give shelter to overwintering butterflies and in spring the new shoots provide food for emerging caterpillars. Because the berries ripen later than other fruit-bearing bushes, they will be eaten eagerly by resident birds and winter visitors. Once established, ivies provide nesting sites for wrens, house sparrows and blackbirds

IVY – ALL YEAR ROUND

AUTUMN Provides nectar for hoverflies and butterflies

WINTER Provides shelter for overwintering butterflies and berries for birds

SPRING Provides nesting site for wrens and blackbirds, young leaves for caterpillars

SUMMER Provides cool roosts and useful nesting sites

ROWAN OR MOUNTAIN ASH
(Sorbus aucuparia)

The mountain ash or rowan is a widespread native tree of woodlands, moors and mountains. With its frothy clusters of flowers and distinctive berries it is one of the basic requirements for the woodland area of a wildlife garden. In the Scottish Highlands, it used to be planted by houses to ward off witchcraft and it is still a popular tree for municipal planting.

TYPE Deciduous tree

FLOWERS Creamy white, late spring, early summer

FRUITS Orange-red berries, autumn. Rich in vitamin C, they make a good jelly

HEIGHT 10–15m (30–50ft)

PLANTING Plant young trees between mid-autumn and early spring

SITE In sun or partial shade. Suitable for a narrow woodland belt or planting individually. Note that it is also tolerant of exposed positions

SOIL Prefers a well-drained, acid soil

CARE No pruning or special care, although it can be coppiced

PROPAGATION Usually seedlings spring up wherever birds deposit the seeds. Can also be grown from seed taken from the berries in autumn

VARIETIES The dwarf rowan (S. aucuparia 'Fastigiata') is a useful variety for the smaller garden. It has the same berries and flowers but grows to only 4m (13ft)

WILDLIFE As the berries start to ripen they are devoured by the resident bird population, particularly blackbirds, well before the winter visitors arrive. The early summer flowers are nectar-rich and rely on insects for their pollination. There are over twenty insect species specifically associated with the rowan tree. Beware of planting the similar-looking Japanese or American rowans, which will not support the same range of insects

WHITEBEAM (Sorbus aria)

The common whitebeam is a close relative of the rowan and another good tree for the wildlife garden. It can reach a height of 25m (80ft) in full maturity, so it is only really suitable for the largest gardens. However, if space is available, this tree does grow on a chalky soil, which the rowan does not, and is equally attractive to birds and insects.

JAPANESE QUINCE
(*Chaenomeles speciosa*)

Originating from China and Japan, C. *speciosa* has a role to play in the wildlife garden. In a small space it can be trained against a fence, where it will start blossoming in late winter in mild districts and bear fruit throughout the autumn.

TYPE Deciduous shrub

FLOWERS Red, pink, white, early to mid-spring

FRUITS Fragrant, yellow-green, edible fruits, autumn

HEIGHT 1.8m (6ft)

SPREAD 1.8m (6ft)

PLANTING Plant bare-root specimens between mid-autumn and early spring. Container-grown plants can be put in at any time except mid-summer

SITE Full sun, trained against a wall or fence

SOIL Any

CARE Prune after flowering, in mid- to late spring

PROPAGATION By semi-hardwood cuttings in late summer

VARIETIES Many garden varieties available. Choose single rather than double forms. 'Apple Blossom' is a popular variety with white flowers tinged with pink

WILDLIFE Spring flowers are attractive to bees and butterflies. Fruit-fall in autumn is eaten by ground-feeding birds (thrushes and blackbirds)

MICHAELMAS DAISY
(*Aster novae-angliae* and *Aster novi-belgii*)

Having been imported from North America around 1710, the Michaelmas daisy is now naturalised in many parts of Britain. The original species went out of favour in the Victorian era, because the flowers were not thought as fine as some of the bolder occupants of the border. Their revival is in some part due to William Robinson who in his book *The Wild Garden* (1870) depicted the Michaelmas daisies growing naturally in New England, and urged readers to find a place for them in the garden.

TYPE Perennial

FLOWERS Violet petals with a yellow central disc. Hundreds of named varieties in shades of pink, blue, red and purple. Early to mid-autumn

HEIGHT Varies according to variety 45cm–1.2m (18in–4ft)

PLANTING Plant young plants 40cm (15in) apart, between mid-autumn and early spring

SITE Open, sunny site, in a flower border or clearing between trees

SOIL Fertile, well drained

CARE Do not allow to dry out during flowering. Divide and replant clumps every two to three years as they take a lot of nourishment from the ground and tend to deteriorate if not moved. Discard any diseased or weak plants. Taller varieties may need supporting with bamboo canes or twigs

PROPAGATION Divide and replant pieces of healthy root taken from the outside of the clump in mid-autumn or late winter

WILDLIFE Provides some of the last nectar of the season, which is particularly important for overwintering butterflies like the tortoiseshells, commas and brimstones

MEADOW SAFFRON
(Colchicum autumnale)

This native flowering bulb is commonly found in grassy meadows and on the edge of woodlands. It is sometimes called the autumn crocus and often confused with the autumn-flowering members of the true crocus family, which look rather similar, although the colchicum's leaves are broader.

TYPE Bulb

FLOWERS Pink, lilac, autumn

HEIGHT Flowers, 15cm (6in); leaves, 25cm (10in)

PLANTING Plant bulbs in late summer/early autumn, 10cm (4in) deep and 20cm (8in) apart. Plant in groups of five or more

SITE Sun or partial shade. In rough grass, woodland edge, borders or containers

SOIL Well drained

CARE No special care needed. Can be left in position for many years

PROPAGATION Divide the clumps in mid-summer; separate and replant the offsets

VARIETIES A white form, C. autumnale 'Album' is also available

WILDLIFE Bumble bees and butterflies visit the brightly coloured flowers to collect nectar and build up food reserves before the onset of winter

TRUE QUINCE

The true quince tree, Cydonia oblonga, is a relative of the ornamental Chaenomeles. Grown for its apple- or pear-shaped fruits, it makes an attractive garden tree. Gather some of the fruit in early autumn, before the first frosts, and leave the remainder for birds and late butterflies.

AUTUMN CROCUS (Crocus speciosus)

The true autumn crocus, although not native, is also worth growing for its bright lilac-blue flowers, heavy with nectar. Planting and cultivation instructions are the same as for the colchicum, although as the crocus has less prominent leaves, the bulbs can be planted closer together, 8–10cm (3–4in). Many garden varieties are available, including a white form, C. speciosus 'Albus'.

PLANNING AND PLANTING A WOODLAND HABITAT

Even the smallest garden can incorporate a woodland habitat. Most of the natural deciduous woods in Britain have been traditionally managed, by coppicing for example. The resulting woodlands are not dark, dense forests, but a series of open glades, copses or woodland-edge habitats, where light is allowed to reach the woodland floor and a wider range of flora and fauna can exist. Beetles, wood wasps, slugs and spiders will make up the insect population, in turn attracting hedgehogs, woodmice, ground-feeding wrens and blackbirds. The native trees should attract a wider number of birds species than before, including jays hunting acorns in autumn, and perhaps nightingales in summer.

SITING THE WOODLAND

It makes sense to utilise what trees are already in the garden and build the woodland around these. The end of the garden is a logical place for a woodland, or along the boundaries. An existing shrubbery would be another starting point – unwanted shrubs could be removed and replaced with species which will attract more wildlife. The orientation of the woodland does not matter too much, although it is best to avoid a south-facing position which might get too much sun.

THE CLASSIC WOODLAND STRUCTURE

An ideal woodland would consist of one or two dominant trees such as beech or oak, underplanted with a canopy of smaller trees like field maple, crab apple and birch. Beneath this would be a shrub layer, composed of hazel, guelder rose and holly. On the woodland floor primroses, bluebells, violets and wild garlic would flourish along with the mosses, lichens and fungi which are essential to the ecology of the woodland.

CHOOSING TREES AND SHRUBS

Think in terms of a three-tier system. The top layer is the larger 'forest' trees. The second layer is made up of small trees and the third layer is the woodland shrubs. In a small garden, only layers two and three are planted – the small trees become the top canopy and the shrubs the underplanting. Choosing native trees and shrubs is always preferable, simply because they support a greater range of insects and associated wildlife. However, any garden species which are useful to wildlife can be included.

WHAT TO LOOK FOR WHEN BUYING TREES

Choose young trees, 1–2m (3–6ft) in height, and look for a strong central upward-growing shoot and a healthy root system. Beware of trees which have had their central growing tip pinched out. This is often done to encourage side shooting, to make the sapling look more like a little tree, but it inhibits natural upward growth. Young trees are best bought from a specialist tree nursery. If possible, choose the specimens yourself rather than have them sent by mail.

RECOMMENDED WOODLAND PLANTS

LAYER 1: LARGE TREES

Beech (*Fagus sylvatica*) I, F
Elm (*Ulmus procera*) I
Oak (*Quercus robur*) I, F
Lime (*Tilia cordata*) I
Hornbeam (*Carpinus betulus*) I
White willow (*Salix alba*) I
Wild cherry (*Prunus avium*) F, N

LAYER 2: SMALL/MEDIUM TREES

Silver birch (*Betula pendula*) I
Downy birch (*Betula pubescens*) I
Field maple (*Acer campestre*) I
Bird cherry (*Prunus padus*) F, N
Crab apple (*Malus sylvestris*) F, N
Rowan (*Sorbus aucuparia*) F

LAYER 3: SHRUBS

Whitebeam (*Sorbus aria*) F
Hawthorn (*Crataegus monogyna*) F, N
Holly (*Ilex aquifolium*) F, C
Hazel (*Corylus avellana*) N, F
Guelder rose (*Viburnum opulus*) F
Dog rose (*Rosa canina*) F, N
Dogwood (*Cornus sanguinea*) I

PLANTING THE WOODLAND

Having chosen the piece of ground where the woodland is to be created, the first task is to clear the area of any rubbish or debris. Lift any unwanted plants and shrubs into pots, ready for replanting elsewhere. There is no need to dig over the ground unless, for example, it is full of builders' rubble. As a general rule, trees and shrubs should be planted 2–3m (6–10ft) apart. Before digging any holes, it is a good idea to have a trial run, placing the saplings in position on top of the earth and moving them around as necessary until you are happy with the layout.

TREE PLANTING

1. Dig a hole about 1m (3ft) across and deep enough to ensure the sapling will sit at the same depth as it did in the nursery. (For container-grown specimens this is the depth of the pot; for bare-root trees, look for a soil mark on the stem.) Loosen the soil in the hole with a fork and add a spadeful of garden compost if available.

2. Use a stout wooden stake which should reach just below where the tree starts to branch. Drive the stake into the centre of the planting hole, as deeply as possible, and hammer in place with a mallet.

3. Part-fill the hole with loose soil and position the tree in the hole, placing a piece of wood across the top of the hole. The old soil mark should be level with the piece of wood. Continue to fill the hole, shaking the tree occasionally to make sure the soil settles between the roots. Once you have filled the hole, tread the soil down firmly, adding more soil if necessary to give a level finish.

4. Use a rubber tree-tie to fix the tree to the stake about 10cm (4in) below any side branches. Choose a tie which has a small rubber buffer attached – this prevents the vulnerable stem from rubbing against the stake.

SHRUB PLANTING

For shrub planting, follow the instructions for planting evergreen shrubs as described in tasks for the month of September.

AFTERCARE

Newly planted trees should be checked regularly during the winter to make sure they have not become dislodged by wind or frost, and that the ties are still in place. As the tree stems thicken, the ties should be loosened to accommodate this growth. In hot or dry weather, trees in their first few years of growth should be watered regularly. It is also important to keep competing seedlings and weeds at bay, to give new trees and shrubs the best chance of survival.

THE WOODLAND FLOOR

You can speed up the process of woodland creation by importing some of the ingredients of a natural woodland floor. Leaf mould will build up gradually as the trees and shrubs grow and shed their leaves, but for the first year, a layer of leaf mould spread around the saplings will enrich the soil. Likewise a layer of coarse bark looks natural, makes a good mulch and keeps weeds at bay.

WOODLAND FLOWERS

It is best to let the trees and shrubs establish themselves for a year or two before planting woodland flowers. At first the gaps will be too large between the trees and there will not be the shade necessary to grow most species. Once the canopy layers have developed, however, there are many woodland plants which can be introduced in the autumn.

WOODLAND MAINTENANCE

During the first five years of a woodland's life, the trees and shrubs will jostle for space and light. By watching the way different species grow, you will soon spot those that need to be halted in their growth or taken out altogether. Coppicing (see tasks for the month of December) is a good way of keeping shrubs in check or, if that seems too drastic, selective pruning of specimens that have outgrown their allotted space will suffice.

RECOMMENDED WOODLAND FLOWERS

Common dog violet (*Viola riviniana*) N

Foxglove (*Digitalis purpurea*) B

Lesser celandine (*Ranunculus ficaria*)

Lily of the valley (*Convallaria majalis*)

Primrose (*Primula vulgaris*) N

Stinking hellebore (*Helleborus foetidus*) B

Wood anemone (*Anemone nemerosa*)

Wood crane's-bill (*Geranium sylvaticum*)

Wood forget-me-not (*Myosotis sylvatica*) B

NOVEMBER

This month is the start of the bird-feeding season and there will be a noticeable return to the garden of resident species which have been feeding further afield. The cold weather can also drive whole flocks of migrants to seek shelter in towns, including large numbers of chaffinches and blackbirds from northern Scandinavia, where winter comes early. The best food source is the long-lasting berries on cotoneaster, pyracantha, berberis and holly but these can disappear literally overnight if a migrating flock of fieldfares descends. Once the natural resources have gone, it is time to dust off the bird table and start winter feeding.

Traditionally, this is bonfire month and whilst there is nothing like the smell of woodsmoke, there are more constructive things to be done with garden rubbish. Compost heaps come in to their own now, providing a way of recycling garden waste and providing homes for slow worms, toads, shrews and woodmice.

The hedgerows are full of native plants in fruit, with many rosehips and berries still intact. Most noticeable this month is the old man's beard or wild clematis, whose fluffy white seedheads may be seen alongside the white globular fruits of the snowberry, an American plant which has become naturalised in Britain.

For the wildlife gardener, the usual tasks of clearing up, cutting back and tidying up the garden should really give way to jobs that will help the resident wildlife make it through the winter ahead. By removing all traces of fallen leaves and dying plants we are taking away vital warmth, food and protective cover for a whole range of insects, birds and mammals. Leave the garden to die back naturally and the creatures in it will have a better chance of surviving until spring.

TASKS FOR THE MONTH

- ☐ Plant spring-flowering bulbs
- ☐ Make leaf mould
- ☐ Keep pond free of leaves
- ☐ Make winter habitats
- ☐ Cut back ivy

NOVEMBER BULB PLANTING

The second phase of bulb planting can take place this month. Snakeshead fritillary (*Fritillaria meleagris*) should be given a place in short grass or on damp soil where it will flower in mid- or late spring. Tulips can also be planted now and will thrive in pots, beds or rockeries. The highly bred garden forms are not as good for insects as the wild tulip (*Tulipa sylvestris*), which grows naturally under hedges and in woodlands, and flowers in mid-spring. Summer-flowering lilies can be planted in an open position with good drainage. There are hundreds of exotic varieties available, but two naturalised species are the tall, pink martagon lily (*Lilium martagon*) and the yellow Pyrenean lily (*Lilium pyrenaicum*). Both are easy to establish and rich in nectar.

PLANTING BULBS

Fritillaria meleagris
PD = 10cm (4in)
DA = 10cm (4in)
Lilium martagon
PD = 10cm (4in)
DA = 23cm (9in)
Lilium pyrenaicum
PD = 13cm (5in)
DA = 23cm (9in)
Tulipa sylvestris
PD = 15cm (6in)
DA = 10cm (4in)

KEY
PD = Planting depth
DA = Distance apart

DEALING WITH AUTUMN LEAVES

A layer of fallen leaves in a woodland area will break down into an ideal growing medium for trees and should not be removed. However it is sensible to rake or sweep up leaves from paths and grassy areas. There are two useful ways of using the collected leaves. The simplest method is just to pile them under hedges or in a spare corner, where they will provide cover for spiders and a host of insects which in turn will provide food for robins and wrens. Piles of leaves are also useful for hibernating hedgehogs. Alternatively, large quantities of leaves can be converted into leaf mould to use as a mulch or to dig into the soil to improve its condition.

Keeping the pond free of leaves

It is better to fish out fallen leaves with a long-handled net than to cover the whole pond with netting. Frogs and toads still need to be able to get in and out and birds to drink and bathe. A few leaves will just decompose and add to the material in the pond, but large quantities from overhanging trees should be removed.

USE LEAVES FOR COMPOST

If there are not enough leaves in the garden to make leaf mould, they can be added to the compost heap, of course.

Making leaf mould

1. Collect leaves with a spring-tined rake or broom – oak and beech make very good leaf mould but any deciduous leaves will do.

2. Pile the leaves into an unused corner of the garden or into a wire netting container. A simple container can be made by driving a single 90cm (3ft) post into the ground and attaching netting in a cylinder shape around it.

3. Firm the leaves down as they accumulate – if they are particularly dry, water the pile with a watering-can.

4. Leave the pile undisturbed for a year, when it will have produced good crumbly leaf mould.

A SIMPLE WIRE-NETTING LEAF MOULD CONTAINER

BONFIRES

As far as wildlife is concerned, bonfires are bad news. Every year, thousands of hedgehogs and small mammals meet their death by climbing into inviting-looking piles of wood, hoping for an undisturbed hibernation. The tradition of burning garden prunings and clippings is a waste of potential sites for overwintering insects, like harvestmen, who actually help gardeners by eating smaller flying insects. The concept of 'rubbish' in a garden needs to undergo a rethink. Decaying plant material is vital to the natural cycle of growth and we should resist the temptation to tidy up too meticulously. Starting a compost heap, or simply piling unwanted wood and vegetation in a corner is a far better use of the garden's resources.

THE FLOWER BED

Borders do tend to look rather tatty at this time of year with few if any flowers, yellowing or fallen leaves and broken stems. The good news is you don't need to do anything about it. Those hollow stems and empty seed pods are providing homes for ladybirds, which if you nurture them over the winter will be ready to feed on the first batch of aphids as they emerge in the spring.

MAKING WINTER HABITATS

Apart from the habitats created by the untidy flower border or hedge bottom, it is possible to create additional overwintering sites specifically to attract wildlife. Choose a corner of the garden which is rarely used, behind a shed or some fairly inaccessible spot which can remain undisturbed for years if necessary. This rough corner should be well away from the house, so that disturbance is kept to a minimum. It also ensures that unwanted wildlife like field mice are not tempted too close to the house (see practical projects for July for advice on establishing an untidy 'no-go' area).

- A pile of logs or old timber will soon be covered in fungi, offering shelter to hedgehogs, woodmice, wrens and possibly foxes.

- A pile of rocks, stones or old paving slabs will harbour insects, possibly slow worms, and offer shelter to hibernating frogs and toads.

- Loosely piled grass clippings or straw will also house insects and ground-feeding birds. They may also attract field mice and shrews.

- A sheet of corrugated iron is an ideal habitat for many types of reptiles and small mammals who will use the 'tunnels' as convenient hiding places.

CUTTING BACK IVY

Mature ivy plants can become overgrown. If this is the case, they can be cut back towards the end of this month, once flowering has finished. Cut all stems to a level of 90cm (3ft) and gently pull away the excess growth.

Plants of the Month

BARBERRY (*Berberis thunbergii*)

One of a whole group of garden shrubs that bears berries well into winter. Not a native plant but a valuable addition to the wildlife garden.

TYPE Deciduous shrub

FLOWERS Pale yellow, spring

FRUITS Scarlet berries from mid-autumn to mid-winter

HEIGHT 1.2m (4ft)

SPREAD 2m (6ft)

PLANTING Plant young specimens between mid-autumn and early spring. For hedging, plants should be set 50cm (20in) apart

SITE In a sunny position in the shrub border or to form a hedge

SOIL Any. Tolerates poor, shallow soils

CARE No regular pruning required. Old plants should have woody stems cut out at ground level in late winter. Hedges can be trimmed if necessary in late summer or early autumn

PROPAGATION From semi-hardwood cuttings in late summer

RELATED *Berberis darwinii* is a more compact species and has bluish-purple berries in autumn

WILDLIFE The mass of small berries can be relied upon to last through the worst part of the winter, providing food for resident and visiting birds. The spiny leaves also give good protection for nesting in spring and summer

FIRETHORN (*Pyracantha*)

Pyracantha is an excellent autumn shrub for its bright berries, but also produces delicate hawthorn-like blossom in early summer. It forms a loosely shaped, informal bush which can be trained on a trellis or wires to grow against a wall.

TYPE Evergreen shrub

FLOWERS White, early summer

FRUITS Orange-red, mid-autumn to late winter

HEIGHT 2.5m (8ft)

SPREAD 3m (10ft)

PLANTING Plant young plants from mid-autumn to early spring

SITE Full sun or shade, will tolerate a north- or east-facing wall

SOIL Fertile, well-drained soil

CARE If grown as a free-standing shrub, no pruning is necessary. Any excessive growth on wall-trained plants can be trimmed back after flowering

PROPAGATION From semi-hardwood cuttings taken in late summer

VARIETIES *P.* 'Orange Glow' is a very vigorous hybrid. *P. rogersiana* 'Flava' has bright yellow berries

WILDLIFE Long-lasting berries provide food for the birds on a first-come, first-served basis. The frothy flowers are also popular with foraging insects

OLD MAN'S BEARD
(*Clematis vitalba*)

This wild clematis gets its name from the white masses that hold the seedheads. It also goes by the name of traveller's joy, perhaps because of its tendency to colonise railway embankments. It is too rampant for the garden proper, but looks magnificent scrambling through a native hedge.

TYPE Deciduous climber

FLOWERS Green-white, mid-summer to early autumn

SEEDHEADS White, feathery masses, mid-autumn to early winter

HEIGHT 15m (50ft). Will grow upwards if supported by a tall tree or shrub, but tends to scramble horizontally

PLANTING Put in new plants between mid-autumn and early spring

SITE Plant next to wall or fence, within an existing hedge or train up through a dead tree. Any aspect. Give new plants support

SOIL Prefers chalk soils

CARE If plant outgrows its space, cut back shoots by two-thirds in late winter

PROPAGATION From semi-hardwood cuttings taken in late summer

WILDLIFE The heavily scented flowers are an excellent nectar source for night-hunting moths, hoverflies and bees. Seedheads are popular with birds

GUELDER ROSE (*Viburnum opulus*)

Grown mainly for its brilliant berries, the guelder rose is one of the best native shrubs for creating an informal hedge or woodland-edge habitat. In the wild, it can be found in damp woodlands.

TYPE Deciduous shrub

FLOWERS Creamy white, early summer

FRUITS Clusters of translucent scarlet-red berries, mid-autumn to early winter

HEIGHT 4m (13ft)

SPREAD 3–4m (10–13ft)

PLANTING Plant young trees between mid-autumn and early spring

SITE Partial or full shade, in shrub border or woodland edge

SOIL Rich, moist soil

CARE No regular pruning required, but dead wood can be thinned out from overgrown shrubs after flowering

PROPAGATION From semi-hardwood cuttings taken in late summer

VARIETIES *V. opulus* 'Compactum' is a better choice for small gardens, reaching only 1.5m (5ft) high

WILDLIFE The berries provide a good early winter food source for birds and the flowers are particularly attractive to hoverflies

STARTING A COMPOST HEAP

Autumn is a logical time of year to start a compost heap, simply because there are lots of prunings and cuttings available, although in fact it can be started at any time of year. A good compost heap has a dual purpose, providing excellent organic matter for the garden and an extra habitat for wildlife.

BIN OR HEAP?

As far as the actual compost is concerned it does not really matter if you use a bin or just make a pile in a corner of the garden. The simplest type of heap is a pyramid shape of material, topped with a piece of old carpet. For a tidier effect, there are several sorts of square bin available made from wire netting or wooden planks. These are preferable to the plastic containers and tumblers which do not allow access to wildlife. One of the simplest and most successful designs is the wooden slatted 'box'

made from spaced planks of wood which allows birds and toads to get to the insects within the compost. Whichever type you choose, make sure it is at least 90cm (3ft) square or bigger, if space allows. Ideally, have two bins, side by side. This makes turning easier, as the material from one can be turned into the other. Alternatively, one can be filled and left to mature whilst the other is being filled with fresh material.

AN EFFECTIVE WOODEN COMPOST BIN DESIGN
TWO BINS SIDE BY SIDE IS THE IDEAL ARRANGEMENT

The compost bin or heap should be out of direct sunlight (to prevent it drying out too quickly). Site it away from overhanging trees, which would drip water directly onto the compost Place it on earth or grass – not concrete – so that worms and insects can enter from the bottom. If possible, raise it slightly off the ground with bricks or wood to allow the air to circulate underneath.

MAKING COMPOST

There are three essentials for making good compost: air, water and nitrogen.

- **Air** needs to be able to circulate around the heap and within it – the secret is not to pack down the material too firmly.

- **Water** – the heap should be moist, but not sodden. If the material is dry it should be sprinkled with water occasionally. A 'lid' of old carpet, thick newspapers or polythene will help to keep out any really heavy downpours.

- **Nitrogen** is the activator that speeds up the decaying process. Any material rich in nitrogen will do: poultry manure, fresh nettles, stable manure, liquid seaweed or fresh grass cuttings.

WARNING
Avoid cooked food scraps or animal products which may attract rats.

COMPOST MATERIALS TO USE

Dead flowers, bedding plants, plant stems

Lawn clippings (in small quantities)

Leaves (in small quantities – large quantities should be piled separately to make leaf mould)

Pondweed

Prunings from trees and shrubs (only if finely shredded)

Raw vegetable matter (such as potato peelings, rotten fruit, sprout stalks)

Tea bags or tea leaves and coffee grounds

Weeds (all except problem perennial weeds like ground elder)

COMPOST MATERIALS TO AVOID

Diseased plants should be burnt. The ash can be added to the heap

Perennial weeds and their roots, particularly ground elder and dandelions

Cooked food

Too many grass clippings. Only add in shallow layers

Woody material that has not been cut into smaller pieces

COMPOSTING METHOD

1. Collect enough material to fill the bin at least half full. If necessary, store in plastic sacks until you have enough. Add the material to the bin in layers of about 15cm (6in). Put the activating material between each layer.

2. Continue adding material until the bin is full. Avoid adding too much of any one type of material and put the 'lid' back on each time to keep in the heat.

3. After about six weeks the compost heap can be turned. Using a fork, turn the material over (into an adjoining bin, if possible), making sure any dry woody material at the edges is brought into the centre. However, if you want to be sure not to disturb any nesting or hibernating wildlife, it is better to leave it unturned. It will still make good compost but it may take a little longer.

4. Sit back and wait. Good compost takes around six months to mature (longer if it is unturned). Meanwhile, start a second heap.

WHAT HAPPENS INSIDE A COMPOST HEAP?

The first things to be broken down are the soft plant leaves and stems – bacteria work on their sugars and produce heat. In the first week the interior of the heap reaches a high temperature, destroying pests and weed seeds and causing the heap to 'steam' on a cold morning. Next the fungi start to work, breaking down the raw material. If you pull back the lid after a couple of weeks you may see the white mycelia of the fungi, lacing their way across the heap. A whole range of microscopic organisms and larger insects now appear, such as spring tails which feed on the fungi and are, in turn, eaten by beetles. Snails, slugs, centipedes, spiders, mites, and eelworms move in and the whole heap becomes a rich feeding ground for frogs, toads, birds and hedgehogs.

WILDLIFE AND THE COMPOST HEAP

Apart from being a food source for wildlife, the heat and moisture provided by the heap make it attractive for nesting. Slow worms have been known to lay their young in the warmth of the heap and grass snakes may lay their clutch of eggs in an undisturbed heap during summer, the young hatching out in early autumn. Hedgehogs do not normally hibernate in compost, as they prefer a drier site. However, they may well 'live' there throughout the summer with a steady supply of slugs on hand. Frogs, toads and newts may utilise the moisture of the heap for hibernation, and toads particularly will not stray far from a good heap all year round.

USING COMPOST

If you decide not to turn the heap, the compost you produce may be a little coarser than the product of a regularly turned heap. It may not be fine enough to use for seed growing and potting, but it will still make an excellent material to dig into the garden as a soil improver, or to use as a mulch.

WHAT WENT WRONG?

· **Compost too slimy** The material is either getting too wet or contains too many grass cuttings. As a general rule, no more than a third of the compost should be grass cuttings.

· **Compost too dry and woody** The material has not been chopped up small enough and contains too much wood from shrubs and trees. Add shallow layers of softer matter (such as some vegetable peelings and grass cuttings) and an 'activator' such as nettles or stable manure.

DECEMBER

This is the traditional time for plants like holly, mistletoe and ivy which carry their own seasonal associations and are steeped in folklore. Holly is said to have power over evil forces and also to protect and provide. This it certainly does – witness the number of creatures seeking out the bush for shelter and food. Ivy is the symbol of everlasting life and friendship. Considering how it continues to cling and climb and provide greenery in every season, it is hard to imagine a more trustworthy garden plant. Mistletoe, on the other hand, is often feared by gardeners as a parasite and destroyer of trees. In fact, although it draws minerals from its host tree, it does not cause serious damage and there are records of mistletoe growing on oak trees for a hundred years or more.

With the first really hard frost of winter, the wildlife garden turns into a sanctuary for foraging birds. The familiar sparrows, robins and blackbirds will be joined by pied wagtails driven in from open parkland and fields, wood pigeons and feral pigeons in search of extra food, as well as continental visitors like blackcaps, redwings, fieldfares and siskins. Wrens, thrushes, dunnocks and tits may all utilise the food and water a garden provides.

Many native mammals are still active in the woods and hedgerows. Foxes will be seeking out food during a cold spell and may visit gardens under cover of darkness. For others, the month is spent underground, like the badgers who line their setts in the autumn and venture out less and less as the weather gets colder. With the last of the deciduous leaves blown to earth, the bones of the wildlife garden are laid bare, revealing shapes it was impossible to see amongst the luxuriant growth of spring and summer. On a frosty day under blue skies, a walk around the garden is one of the most refreshing and enjoyable ways to end the year.

TASKS FOR THE MONTH

☐ Start feeding birds

☐ Keep pond free of ice

☐ Plant bare-root roses

☐ Coppice trees and shrubs

BIRD FEEDING

Start to put out food for the birds this month. There should still be some natural food available in the form of berries, but flower seeds and windfallen fruit are finished. Regular feeding encourages birds to get into the habit of visiting the bird table, which means they are more likely to survive winter and use the garden to breed in the spring. Unsalted nuts, seeds, dried fruit, grated cheese and apples are all acceptable foods. (See December's practical project for advice on choosing bird tables and feeders.)

KEEPING POND FREE OF ICE

The weather this month is often not as harsh as expected. However, if a freeze does come, it is important to keep ponds and water sources free of ice and easily available to wildlife (see tasks for the month of January for methods).

THINGS TO REMEMBER ABOUT ROSES

Container-grown roses from garden centres can be planted at any time of year as long as the ground is not frozen or waterlogged. Shrub roses may be pruned in the first spring after planting.

PLANTING BARE-ROOT SHRUB ROSES

If the weather is still frost free, bare-root shrub roses ordered from nurseries can be planted this month. The planting method applies to: *Rosa rugosa*, *Rosa canina*, *Rosa rubiginosa* and *Rosa glauca*. If the ground is frozen it is better to wait until late winter or early spring.

Plant the roses as soon as possible after they arrive. If this is not possible, the roots should be buried in a shallow trench in the garden and watered. They can be left for several months like this before replanting. Shrub roses should be planted 1.5m (5ft) away from the next shrub.

1. Using secateurs, cut off any leaves, flower buds or damaged stems (make any cuts to an outward-facing bud).

2. Dig a hole to fit the shape of the roots – usually this is no more than 25cm (10in) deep, but may be up to 60cm (2ft) across.

3. Mix some of the soil from the hole with organic manure or garden compost and spread a 5cm (2in) layer of the mixture at the bottom of the hole.

4. Spread out the roots in the hole, adjusting the planting depth, if necessary, to ensure that the junction between the rootstock and the stem will be level with the surrounding soil. Fill with ordinary soil and tread lightly, adding a final layer of soil as needed.

COPPICING TREES AND SHRUBS

The ancient skill of coppicing has been practised at least since Anglo-Saxon times and possibly longer. As a traditional form of woodland management, it served two important functions: to provide a renewable source of wood for fuel and fencing and to allow selected trees space to grow to full maturity for subsequent cropping as timber. It also had a secondary (probably unintentional) effect which was to let in light to the woodland floor, regenerating the plants and flowers growing there, and their dependent wildlife. Coppice shoots also provided food for deer, which may or may not have been welcome depending on the wood's purpose. The word 'copse' denotes a wood that was once coppiced.

It is not necessary to have acres of land or a full-blown wood to practise coppicing in the garden. In fact, if space is restricted, coppicing native shrubs and trees allows gardeners to grow a greater range of species than there would normally be room for.

What is coppicing?

Coppicing means cutting the tree down to ground level, to allow new shoots to spring up from the base. Far from killing the tree, this practice encourages the tree's natural power of regeneration, whereby it will throw up new poles of wood, year after year.

Why coppice?

A coppiced woodland, even on a small scale, allows a broad range of plants, birds, mammals and insects to co-exist. The main, tall-growing trees such as oak, beech and ash provide the upper canopy for nesting birds. This is underplanted with a layer of smaller trees and shrubs which may be coppiced; white willow, wych elm, hornbeam, bird cherry, hazel and lime. Beneath this, on the woodland floor, primroses,

bluebells and other woodland plants flourish in the leaf mould and dappled shade provided by the trees above. In the garden, coppiced trees will not produce blossom or berries, but the young leaves and shoots produced in the spring will support a new generation of butterfly caterpillars and other leaf-eating insects.

How to coppice

- **Year 1:** Use pruners for small stems and a strong pruning saw for thicker ones. Cut the stems to several centimetres (a few inches) above ground level.

- **Subsequent years:** Depending on how fast the different species grow, some coppicing can take place every winter. It is usual to rotate the cropping, so that there is a succession of available wood. Each individual tree or shrub should be left between five and seven years before coppicing again, allowing it to form a medium-sized shrub. If the wood is not needed for a specific purpose, trees and shrubs may be coppiced whenever they outgrow their allotted space. As the years go by, a coppiced tree will start to form a stool. Shoots thrown up from this stool should be cut back to within 5–8cm (2–3in) of this old wood.

COPPICING

SHRUBS AND TREES SUITABLE FOR COPPICING

Ash (*Fraxinus excelsior*)

Common alder (*Alnus glutinosa*)

Dogwood (*Cornus sanguinea*)

Elder (*Sambucus nigra*)

Field maple (*Acer campestre*)

Goat willow (*Salix caprea*)

Hazel (*Corylus avellana*)

Hornbeam (*Carpinus betulus*)

Oak (*Quercus robur*)

Small-leaved lime (*Tilia cordata*)

Sweet Chestnut
(*Castanea sativa*)

White willow (*Salix alba*)

Wych elm (*Ulmus glabra*)

POLLARDING

Pollarding is another traditional method of restricting the size of trees and letting more light reach the ground. Instead of cutting the stems to ground level, the trunk is cut at a height of 2–5m (6–15ft) leaving a permanent trunk called a 'bolling'. New shoots then sprout from the bolling, keeping the wood out of reach of animals until it is cut for use. It is best to select a young tree for pollarding, before the trunk is too large – older trees need to be done professionally. Pollarding is usually carried out on isolated trees, or those in formal rows, not those in the centre of a wood where it would be difficult to work. Poles of wood can be cut from the tree every year, but re-pollarding should only take place every ten to twenty years.

POLLARDING

USING COPPICED WOOD

The poles are also extremely useful for fence posts, tree stakes, hurdle making and wattle work.

Plants of the Month

HOLLY (*Ilex aquifolium*)

Native to most parts of Britain and literally hundreds of varieties can be found. An excellent wildlife tree to plant on the edge of the woodland or as a boundary hedge.

TYPE Evergreen tree

FLOWERS White, spring

FRUITS Red berries from late autumn to late winter usually on female trees – there needs to be a male tree nearby to ensure fertilisation

HEIGHT 5–8m (15–25ft)

SPREAD 2.5–4m (8–13ft)

PLANTING Plant young specimens in autumn or winter (if the ground is not frozen). Add compost or manure to the planting hole. For hedging, choose plants about 45cm (18in) high and space them at 60cm (24in) intervals

SITE Sun or shade. Variegated forms will have better colouring in a sunny position. Very tolerant of pollution and salt spray; useful for screening in coastal or built-up areas

SOIL Any

CARE Keep well watered, especially through the summer. Pinch out shoots of new hedging in first spring after planting. When fully grown, trim hedges annually in early spring (after berries are finished but before nesting begins). Trees do not need regular pruning

PROPAGATION By cuttings taken in late summer

WILDLIFE One of the best trees for nesting birds, because of the protection offered by the spiky leaves. The berries last well into the winter, providing food for birds, particularly fieldfares and redwings

HAWTHORN (*Crataegus monogyna*)

Also known as May blossom, the common hawthorn is a much-loved native shrub. From late summer to autumn, its scarlet berries provide food for visiting birds.

TYPE Deciduous shrub or tree

FLOWERS White, sometimes tinged pink, early summer

FRUITS Red berries, mid-autumn to early winter

HEIGHT Up to 8m (25ft)

SPREAD 5m (15ft)

PLANTING Plant young trees between mid-autumn and early spring. For a hedge, use 45cm (18in) high plants, 30cm (12in) apart

SITE Sun or partial shade. As a screen, hedge or planted at the edge of a woodland belt

SOIL Any

CARE Trees that get too large can be cut back hard in mid-summer. Trim hedges annually, after flowering and after any nesting birds have vacated – usually by late summer or early autumn

PROPAGATION From seed sown in autumn

WILDLIFE Birds feed on the berries in late autumn and winter; the dense tangle of thorns makes an excellent nesting site in spring. In early summer, its sweetly scented blossom attracts insects, with over a hundred species associated with it

MIDLAND HAWTHORN
(*Crataegus laevigata*)

The Midland hawthorn is somewhat smaller than the common hawthorn, reaching only 5m (15ft), and a good choice where space is limited. The flowers are purely white and scented and it can be distinguished from *C. monogyna* by the berries, which have two or three pips instead of one.

WINTER CELEBRATIONS

Evergreens have special significance at this time of year, retaining their foliage and colour when other plants are losing theirs. Ivy, holly and mistletoe bear fruit in the dead of winter so don't forget to share it with the garden's creatures. By all means bring boughs of holly and mistletoe into the house for the festive season, but afterwards put them into a corner of the garden to wither naturally. Blackbirds, thrushes and ground-feeding wrens will pick off any left-over berries.

MISTLETOE
(*Viscum album*)

This native plant is found growing on the branches of deciduous trees, especially apples, poplars, willows, limes and sometimes oaks. It is usually planted by birds feeding on the berries and wiping their beaks against the bark of nearby trees.

TYPE Evergreen, parasitic shrub

FLOWERS Yellow-green, late winter to mid-spring

FRUITS Semi-translucent white berries, mid-autumn to mid-winter

SPREAD Clumps up to 60cm (2ft) across

PROPAGATION In mid-winter take berries from a garden tree. (Don't use shop-bought sprigs which may be imported species, not suited to growing in Britain.) Push the berries under a flap of cut bark or into existing crevices. It is best to try this on a tree of the same type from which the parent plant was taken. Germination will take three months and berries will not appear on the new plant for seven years

WILDLIFE The white, globular berries are a good food source for birds. The sticky pulp surrounding the seeds sticks to their beaks and in an endeavour to remove it, the seeds are wiped onto the trunk of the next tree, getting trapped in the grooves of the bark

CHOOSING A BIRD TABLE OR FEEDER

There is a bewildering choice of bird tables and feeders available from garden centres and by mail order. Some are very high-tech in design, with shoots, perches, roofs and ledges in chrome and plastic. These seem rather elaborate for what is basically a straightforward job – presenting food to the birds in a place where they can eat safely and where humans can watch them do so. In fact, research shows that birds are completely indifferent to what the table or feeder looks like, as long as they can reach the food safely and easily.

The simple, traditional wooden bird table is still a favourite for a natural-looking garden but, to be functional, it should incorporate certain basic features. A raised rim around the edge of the tray is useful to prevent food from being knocked off, and there should be a small gap in this rim to allow rainwater to drain away. The base must be sturdy enough to stop it being knocked over by pets, children, or indeed foxes searching for food. A roof is not essential but it does keep the food dry and protected from snow falls.

HANGING FEEDERS

These feeders are designed to be hung from the table, or from a window ledge, wall, or fence. Many birds prefer this kind of acrobatic feeding, particularly tits, finches and even sparrows. Feeders containing nuts are usually cylinders of wire mesh or metal spirals. Models with a spring-action bottom plate are a good idea, as it prevents nuts becoming trapped at the bottom where they can be left to rot. If your model does not have this feature, make sure you periodically take down the feeder and scrape out any old nuts that have become stuck to the bottom.

WINDOW FEEDERS

A feeder that fixes directly to the window is one of the best ways to see birds at close quarters. These devices are especially useful for people who are housebound, but also practical for flat dwellers with no access to a garden. Again there are many designs available, but a simple one made of clear plastic that sticks to the window with suckers is probably as good as any.

WHERE TO SITE A BIRD TABLE

The feeding area should be in clear view of one or more windows in the house, where everyone can see it. Birds seem to get used to human activity so it can be placed quite close to the house. Make sure it is a couple of metres (a good few feet) away from dense cover, where cats or other predators could hide.

MAKING A LOG FEEDER TO ATTRACT WOODPECKERS

Woodpeckers are frequently seen in gardens, pecking away in the crevices in tree bark for their insect food. Take a piece of rotten log, make a few deep holes in the wood and stuff them full of lard or suet, mixed with bird seed. Suspend the log from the branch of a tree to attract both greater and lesser spotted woodpeckers. Incidentally, the green woodpecker spends more time on the ground than other woodpeckers and may not feed on the log.

MAKING A SIMPLE BIRD TABLE

Detailed instructions for making bird tables can be obtained from the Royal Society for the Protection of Birds (see Resources). However, a basic table is easy and cheap to make.

1. Use an old wooden tray with a lip around it and nail or screw it to a stout post about 1.2–1.5m (4–5ft) high.

2. Nail or screw the bottom of the post to a large square of wood, to form the base.

3. Add pieces of wood of equal length and with their ends cut at angles around the base of the table for stability.

4. Position the table on level ground, weighting it with stones if necessary.

WHO FEEDS WHERE?

To ensure that all the birds in the garden are catered for, it is a good idea to have three types of feeding situation: a table, several hanging feeders, and also food on the ground. (For more details on what to feed, see tasks for the month of January.)

Table-feeding birds

Robins, house sparrows, tree sparrows, collared doves, chaffinches, bramblings, wood pigeons, bullfinches, greenfinches.

Acrobatic-feeding birds

Blue tits, great tits, coal tits, siskins, nuthatches, house sparrows, tree sparrows, bullfinches, greenfinches.

Ground-feeding birds

Blackbirds, thrushes, dunnocks, wrens, fieldfares, redwings.

TRAY

POST

BASE

GOOD HYGIENE

It is vital to keep the bird table clean. If not, bacteria can build up and cause outbreaks of disease among birds. Scrape off droppings and any uneaten food daily and scrub down with a mild disinfectant solution every few weeks.

TOP TEN GARDEN BIRDS

The ten most common birds in British gardens according to the most recent Big Garden Birdwatch conducted by the RSPB are:

1 House sparrow

2 Blue tit

3 Starling

4 Wood pigeon

5 Blackbird

6 Robin

7 Goldfinch

8 Great tit

9 Magpie

10 Chaffinch

CONTAINER GARDENING FOR WILDLIFE

It is quite possible to entice wildlife into even the most unpromising paved areas by utilising containers. Several mini-habitats can be created by growing a carefully selected range of trees, shrubs and flowers in pots, tubs, window boxes and hanging baskets.

If the space is enclosed by walls or high fences, it is important to let the passing wildlife know that this area is a source of food and shelter. Aim to add height and greenery with a small native tree grown in a good-sized wooden barrel and add one or two berry-bearing shrubs. Clothe the walls in climbers for nesting birds and introduce nectar-rich flowers for the insects. Finally, put up a nesting box amongst the climbers and find a place for a feeding table in winter and a bird bath in summer. Despite the lack of grass and full-size trees, a surprising range of creatures will begin to inhabit this new garden.

DON'T FORGET HERBS

Herbs are amongst the most useful wildlife plants, including borage, mint, chives and rosemary, and are ideally suited to container growing. Do allow them to flower though, even at the expense of a continuous supply of leaves for cooking.

STEP-BY-STEP CONTAINER PLANTING

1. Make sure the container has adequate drainage holes and that they are free of obstruction.

2. Put a layer of broken clay pots or crockery over the base of the container.

3. Half fill with a multi-purpose potting compost.

4. Place the plants in position and fill around the root balls with more compost. Press down firmly.

5. Water well and add more compost if necessary, to bring the level to 2.5cm (1in) below the rim of the container.

FOUR-SEASON WINDOW BOX

Try planting a window box with the following selection of evergreens, perennials, bulbs and bedding plants, for an all-the-year-round display:

WINTER Ivy, hellebores, snowdrops

SPRING Ivy, yellow crocus and grape hyacinths

SUMMER Ivy, white alyssum and dwarf lavender

AUTUMN Ivy, meadow saffron

SOURCES OF WATER

Don't forget water for a container garden; a large plant pot saucer will do as a source of water for wildlife, or make use of an old sink, plastic tub or washing up bowl as a bird bath.

WILDLIFE FRIENDLY YARD
To boost the wildlife habitat in a concrete yard, make a pile of logs in one corner. As the wood begins to break down, it will house beetles, spiders and slugs – gnat food for birds. The cool, damp habitat may be secluded enough to offer daytime cover to a toad, or frogs and newts from a nearby pond.

RECOMMENDED PLANTS

TREES

Rowan (*Sorbus aucuparia* 'Fastigiata')
Dwarf form (3m/10ft); flowers for insects and berries for birds

Willow (*Salix caprea* 'Pendula')
Weeping form (3m/10ft); catkins for insects, young leaves for caterpillars

SHRUBS

Buddleia (*Buddleia davidii*)
(3m/10ft) Nectar flowers for butterflies

Cotoneaster '*Hybridus Pendulus*'
(3m/10ft) Berries and flowers

Hawthorn (*Crataegus monogyna*)
(5m/15ft) Can be pruned hard to keep it within bounds. Secure nesting site for birds; berries and flowers

Holly (*Ilex aquifolium*)
(5m/15ft) A male and female bush are needed to be sure of berries. Nesting cover for birds

Lavender (*Lavandula angustifolia*)
Scented bee flowers

CLIMBERS

Honeysuckle (*Lonicera periclymenum*)
Summer wall/fence cover; nectar flowers

Ivy (*Hedera helix*)
All-year-round wall/fence cover; nectar flowers

FLOWERS FOR NECTAR

Alyssum

Candytuft (*Iberis*)

Nasturtium (*Tropaeolum majus*)

Nicotiana

Night-scented stock
(*Matthiola bicornis*)

Pot marigold (*Calendula officinalis*)

GARDEN PLANS

Every garden is different and every gardener wants something slightly different from their own space. Some gardens only need a few modifications to make them more attractive to wildlife; others, particularly brand new gardens, can be designed specifically to include all the main wildlife habitats. Designing a garden from scratch need not be as daunting as it at first seems. Look at as many other gardens as possible (particularly neighbouring ones which are the same shape and size) and make notes of features you would definitely want to include (use the checklist of essential features for wildlife provided in tasks for the month of January). It is a good idea to take a photograph of the garden, perhaps taken from an upstairs window to give an overview. This photograph can then be used as the basis of your plan – by laying over pieces of tracing paper, features can be drawn in to build up a picture of what the finished garden might look like.

TRADITIONAL WILDLIFE GARDEN
A SMALL RECTANGULAR PLOT IS QUITE SIMPLY ADAPTED TO THE NEEDS OF WILDLIFE

KEY

1 Compost bin provides organic material and a good hunting ground for insect-eating birds and toads.

2 Flowering meadow supplies nectar for a wide range of butterflies.

3 Piles of logs and leaves encourage beetles and other small insects – another food source for birds and small mammals like hedgehogs.

4 Shrub border including native species like hazel and berry-bearing species like berberis and cotoneaster.

5 A pond is vital for breeding frogs and newts and as a water supply for birds and mammals.

6 Marshy ground adjoining the pond extends the plant species and offers cover to young amphibians.

7 Flower border with nectar-rich and seed-bearing species will be visited by moths, bees and butterflies, and birds in the autumn.

8 Bird table attracts birds to feed in the garden in winter and, hopefully, return to nest in spring.

9 Buddleia bush has a place in every wildlife garden for the huge numbers of butterflies it attracts.

KEY

1 Flower border crammed with nectar plants for bees and butterflies.

2 Nesting box on a north- or east-facing wall for small birds.

3 Climbers in pots, such as clematis or honeysuckle, attract a range of insects.

4 Herbs in pots by the back door are handy for the kitchen and for passing bees and butterflies.

5 A formal pond can be softened with poolside planting to offer cover to young frogs and toads.

6 Compost bin is cleverly hidden behind shrubs, but still accessible to wildlife.

7 Meadow is situated away from the house, giving an undisturbed natural area at the back of the garden.

8 Trees can be incorporated in larger gardens as part of the 'woodland' belt.

9 Mixed hedgerow of native species makes an excellent 'wildlife' corridor and an effective boundary between you and the neighbours.

A GARDEN FOR URBAN WILDLIFE

A WILDLIFE GARDEN CAN RETAIN SOME FORMAL ELEMENTS, PARTICULARLY IN THE AREAS CLOSEST TO THE HOUSE.

WILDLIFE ORGANISATIONS

Barn Owl Trust
www.barnowltrust.org.uk

Bat Conservation Trust
www.bats.org.uk

British Dragonfly Society
www.british-dragonflies.org.uk

British Trust for Ornithology
www.bto.org

Butterfly Conservation
www.butterfly-conservation.org

Royal Horticultural Society
www.rhs.org.uk

Royal Society for the
Protection of Birds
www.rspb.org.uk

The Hedgehog
Preservation Society
www.britishhedgehogs.org.uk

The Wildlife Trusts
www.wildlifetrusts.org

Woodland Trust
www.woodlandtrust.org.uk

FURTHER READING

RHS Companion to Wildlife Gardening Chris Baines (Frances Lincoln 2016)

Sowing Beauty: Designing Flower Meadows from Seed James Hitchmough (Timber Press 2017)

The Flowering of Britain Richard Mabey and Tony Evans (Pbk. Chatto & Windus 1989)

The Illustrated Flora of Britain and Northern Europe Marjorie Blamey and Christopher Grey-Wilson (Hodder & Stoughton 1989)

Trees and Woodland in the British Landscape Oliver Rackham (Dent 1990)

Wildlife Gardening Kate Bradbury (Bloomsbury 2019)

INDEX

ISBN-13: 9781446309537 paperback
ISBN-13: 9781446382103 EPUB
ISBN-13: 9781446382097 PDF

Publishing Director: Ame Verso
Commissioning Editor: Freya Dangerfield
Managing Editor: Jeni Chown
Editors: Jessica Cropper and Verity Muir
Project Editor: Cheryl Brown
Proofreader: Jane Trollope
Head of Design: Anna Wade
Designer: Sam Staddon
Illustrations: Yevheniia Lytvynovych
Additional Illustrations: Avis Murray
Production Manager: Bev Richardson

This book has been printed on paper from
approved suppliers and made from pulp
from sustainable sources.

MIX
Paper from
responsible sources
FSC® C012521

Printed in China through Asia Pacific Offset for:
David and Charles, Ltd
Suite A, Tourism House, Pynes Hill, Exeter, EX2 5WS

10 9 8 7 6 5 4 3 2 1

David and Charles publishes high-quality books on
a wide range of subjects. For more information visit
www.davidandcharles.com.

Follow us on Instagram by searching for
@dandcbooks_wellbeing

Layout of the digital edition of this book may vary
depending on reader hardware and display settings.